Overcoming the Heart of Darkness

Missionary Journeys
Home & Abroad

Desiree Campbell

The Rose of Sharon Ministry

Overcoming the Heart of Darkness
Missionary Journeys Home & Abroad

ISBN-13: 978-1517190958

All profits from the sale of this book help support the
Rose of Sharon ministry

Email address:
roseofsharon.campbell@gmail.com

Postal address:
P.O. Box 11714
Centurion
0046
Gauteng
South Africa

Front cover image credit: Olga Nikitina/123RF
Back cover image credit: Abstract412/123RF *2

Dedication

To my darling husband, Gavin, whose faith is an inspiration to me. I could never have written this book without him. Thank you for all your love, support, and encouragement.

To my daughter Deanne who has given up so much of her mother to allow me to do what I feel the Lord has called me to do. Thank you.

Table of Contents

Introduction...7

Chapter

1 – Background and Early Years.................................11

2 – Not All Was Plain Sailing.................................27

3 – Beginning of the Rural Work.................................43

4 – Travelling Further Afield.................................61

5 – Kwa Zulu Natal.................................71

6 –The Gospel River Ministry.................................81

7 – Clandestine Ministry in China.................................87

8 – Israel: Not All It Seems.................................95

9 – Lay Your All on the Altar of Sacrifice.................................105

10 – Leaving All Things Dear.................................115

11 – "I'll Take the High Road..." 123

12 – First Port of Call: The Uists.................................131

13 – Revival Country: Lewis.................................141

14 –Sailing the High: Seas-Orkney and Westray.................................151

15 – Shetland Safari.................................161

16 – Open Your Ears and Listen! Keswick.................................171

17 – Over the Sea to Skye.................................179

18 – "Donald Where's Yer Troosers?" Glasgow.................................189

19 – Violence and Blessing: Ireland.................................207

20 –Into the Wilds of London.................................221

21 – Full Circle.................................231

Epilogue.................................239

Introduction

Can it really be 25 years? It doesn't seem real that for the past 25 years, I have been working for the Lord in the Rose of Sharon Ministries. So much has happened with so many adventures, so much joy—and a fair amount of pain! To God alone be the glory for keeping and sustaining me on this walk with Him.

This book came into being by the leading of the Lord and the encouragement of many folks who kept saying, "You should write a book!" One morning I awoke and felt an internal nudge and a quiet still voice saying, "Now, the time is now". I have no idea why now, but who can know the mind of God, whose ways are so much higher than ours?

We are a faith-based mission and there are no spare funds for a book project such as this. However, when my mother passed she left a small legacy and I am using it to tell the story of some of the wondrous things our Saviour has done for us. My prayer is that these stories from the mission field will inspire and bless you, and the name of Jesus will be lifted high and He will be praised.

There are so many folks out there who need to be thanked because this book would never have come into being without them. First, to my sister Heather, who, in the face of her own difficulties and struggles has been a pillar of strength to me. Bless you for your steadfast love.

Special thanks to my best and dearest friend, Julie Whitlock. Julie, you have walked the extra mile a hundred times over and have shared all my joys and all my pain. Thank you for always being there for me.

Thank you to Rob and Julie Whitlock, Roy Witelson and Trish Schmidt who have all served on the Board of Trustees of Rose of Sharon in South Africa. And thank you to Jacqui Lindsay, John and Jill Taylor, Frank Hartley and Ishie MacDonald who serve on the Board of Trustees in Scotland. Gavin and I are indebted to you all for your faithful support and prayers over many years.

There are so many of you who make the work of Rose of Sharon sustainable, and without you we would not be able to continue our calling. I cannot mention you all by name but wish to express my most sincere gratitude to our family, friends and supporters. Thank you for giving to the Lord and for partnering with us in spreading the Gospel.

I apologise for not being able to mention you by name, but as John 21:25 says, "Jesus did many things as well. If every one of them were written down, I suppose that even the whole world would not have room for the books that would be written."

A special thanks to my wonderful, God-given editor, D.L. Hughes, without whom this book would not have seen the light of day. Don, your belief in me, your wisdom, knowledge and guidance has been valuable. Thank you for being patient and encouraging when I have been out of my depth. You have picked me up and steered me in the right direction. Thank you.

Shall we all climb aboard the travelling Campbell bus and let the adventure begin? Welcome to you one and all....

Chapter 1

Background and Early Years

"Get out! Be gone with you!" screamed the big, burly group of Afrikaans men, through the locked, barred front door of our home. "You will leave now if you know what's good for you! You are not wanted here!"

"What now Lord? Where to from here?" we cried silently. Where were we to go? We had no idea.

Since the early 1990's, my husband Gavin and I have been involved in spreading the Gospel, church planting and caring for the underprivileged in our country of South Africa. When the ministry began, it was in the era of the abhorrent and evil apartheid system of discrimination against people of colour. At that time, there were very few mission organisations working in the informal settlements springing up in and around the major cities of South Africa.

Most of the folks living in these shanty towns came from neighbouring countries, or parts of our own country, looking for work. There was a belief that if they could reach Johannesburg they would become wealthy. This was far from the truth, of course. These poor folks found themselves with no homes and no work.

This led to terrible poverty and entire families lived in one tiny shack made up of little more than plastic, cardboard or some corrugated iron sheets. Pigs would snuffle through piles of rotting rubbish strewn thoughtlessly about, while nauseating raw sewage trickled down the makeshift dirt roads.

With no running water, children drudged through mud and filth to the nearest tap, pushing stolen supermarket trol-

Millions of people living in abject poverty in Shanty Towns.

leys filled with battered containers, to fetch water for the family's needs. The air would often be thick with acrid smoke from the many cooking fires as there was no electricity.

Squawking chickens, mangy barking dogs, crying, hungry children and angry shouting adults were common sounds. Alcohol abuse was rife and violent crime was the order of the day.

We wanted to reach out with the Gospel to these people and to meet their temporal needs as much as we could. As the Bible says, "Suppose a brother or sister is without clothes and daily food. If one of you says to him "Go, I wish you well; keep warm and well fed," but does nothing about his physical needs, what good is it? "(NIV, James 2: 15-16).

We craved to share the Gospel with them but they were too hungry and needy to listen. Material needs had to be met with spiritual ones. We started fetching day old bread from supermarkets and bakeries and distributing these in local areas where needs were the greatest.

The supermarkets then began to give us other food stuffs; fruit and vegetables that were beyond their sell-by dates and stale cakes from the bakery. We would drive around to the service delivery area of the supermarket where we would be confronted with cream cakes tossed carelessly on top of meat pies. Vegetables that were still edible would be amongst slimy rotting ones that were beyond being salvageable. Rotting fruit, seeping with smelly juices, would cover firm fruit. Carefully and methodically, we cleaned and sorted through the piles of food, separating what could be eaten from the rest. This would then be given in large quantities to those who had so little. Often we too partook of this fare when we were in need.

It was not safe to travel in some informal settlements because of the volatile political climate. It was just before the

1994 elections and our country was in turmoil. Most people were expecting a bloodbath, but God in His mercy intervened and this did not occur.

This did not negate the violence that was being perpetrated throughout the land, which was criminally, not politically, motivated. Most of these shanty towns were run by civic leaders and their cronies who kept a tight control on all that was happening within that particular settlement. Gun totting thugs would monitor all who came and went in their designated area. We had to get permission from these leaders before being allowed into a shanty town to help those in need. Certain areas were more open to aid than others, and it was here that we saw God opening doors.

Wheiler's Farm was one such informal settlement. It was situated on the southern outskirts of the city of Johannesburg. It was tightly controlled by civic leaders and if you had a white skin, you stayed well away. A number of white folk in the region had been shot. It was known as a no-go area.

We had a pastor friend who was taken ill and in a hospital in Soweto, and Gavin went to visit him. Soweto, is a huge, largely African settlement in Johannesburg. It is disadvantaged, but does not reach the same level of deprivation we saw in the shanty towns. There were some tarred roads and running water. The sights were still heart breaking. We would see rickety horse drawn carts being pulled by tired, undernourished horses, often ribs showing, plodding relentlessly on. They pulled wagons laden with huge amounts of junk being taken to the scrap metal dealers. Men, or young boys, pulled wagons filled with plastic bottles or reams of scrap paper for recycling. Children loitered aimlessly in the streets, with nothing to do, and dogs would scratch through muck looking for scraps to eat.

A small boy collecting recyclable waste.

While at the hospital, a little old African lady came up to Gavin and handed him a note. He did not know this woman, but she had seen him in one of the settlements where we were working.

The letter was from the civic leaders in Wheiler's Farm asking Gavin to feed the children at the school. This was unheard of and a shock. So, with some trepidation we loaded up the car with discarded loaves of bread from the local bakery and headed into Wheiler's Farm.

We had no sooner entered when we were stopped by armed men who were clearly agitated by our presence. Gavin quickly pulled out the letter from the civic leaders, waving it frantically in their faces. They snatched the letter and read it.

After some nervous deliberation we were surrounded and forcibly escorted to their headquarters. We were hurriedly ushered inside a makeshift rickety building. The civic leaders sat on boxes, plastic cold drink crates or broken chairs. They wanted us to give them the bread for distribution. Gavin bravely stood up to them, insisting that we be allowed to deliver the bread to the school, thereby making sure it was given to those for whom it was intended. After tense discussion it was finally and reluctantly agreed that we could do so. For the next nine months we went to the makeshift, cardboard shanty school at least three times a week, taking loaves of bread and other supplies we had available.

School could hardly be the correct term to use for the building or for what went on in there. The structure itself was far from safe. It was erected mainly from large sheets of hardboard and bits of plastic. The school had no supplies. Four groups of children gathered in one large room. Each group, according to their age, faced a separate wall. The children sat on the dirt floor and were taught by unqualified volunteer ladies. There were no books, pens or paper that we saw. Some children were so hungry they couldn't concentrate on their school work. In dire need, mothers would wrap strips of cloth tightly around little swollen tummies in an attempt to alleviate hunger pains.

Coming and going in these areas was always a tense time because of trigger happy thugs. We never knew for certain whom we could trust. After unloading supplies one day, we were once again confronted with armed men who insisted we accompany them. We were taken back to the civic leaders who told us they had been watching us and saw all we did. We were then told, "We know you are from the church, so if you want to come and play church here, you may do so".

Other white people could not get in, but we were invited to plant a church. Oh, the goodness of our Lord! This started

Grace, a faithful volunteer, outside her shack.

a seven year pastorate for Gavin. The little old lady who gave Gavin the letter became like a mother to us. Her name was Grace and she was a wonderful woman who loved the Lord with all her heart. She had a little shanty house in Wheiler's Farm. At the back of her shack we erected a tarpaulin structure that served as the church. Sunday by Sunday we would hold services there, cramming as many as three hundred adults in such a tiny space where there wasn't even room enough to sit down. There were no windows and no chairs. A combination of heat, flies and cockroaches made the experience far from comfortable!

We also established a place of safety for the children. School would end around one or two in the afternoon and there was nothing for the children to do. They would hang about listlessly in the dusty dirt roads thoroughly bored with nothing to occupy their time. There was always the threat of the young ones being snatched by witch doctors. The witch doctors highly prized children's body parts to put into their black magic potions. Many children were snatched for this purpose. We were able to procure some climbing frames, swings and a slide. These we placed next to the shanty church and Grace watched over the children in the afternoons.

The witch doctor is an acceptable part of daily living for most African people. They consulted them for all manner of reasons, from health issues to placing a curse upon an enemy. The witch doctors had "Muti" shops where they would sell their magic potions to cure all and sundry. Adverts could be found on boards tied to street lamps promoting potions for just about any ailment, or curse. The biggest problem we faced with the witch doctors was their recommendation in relation to a cure for HIV/AIDS.

AIDS had become a huge challenge in South Africa, but at that time our government was not willing to acknowledge the problem. They did not have a plan to distribute anti-retroviral drugs. The witch doctors claimed that to be cured of AIDS, a man needed to have intercourse with a virgin. This was the start of a huge spate of rapes on innocent little babies and small children. Infants as young as six weeks old were raped to death. We tried our best to protect the children in the shanty towns by making places of safety available to them, informing them of the situation, and teaching them to be vigilant.

The socio-economic and associated problems in these areas were huge and sometimes insurmountable. Most families lived in a tiny one-roomed shelter made of either plastic or cardboard, corrugated iron sheeting, or a mixture of all three. The shacks had no floors. Some folks managed to procure old carpeting which was laid on the bare sand floor, and others just lived with a dirt floor. Beds were rare and most children slept on the ground. Because everyone in the family lived in the one room, children were exposed to adult activities from a very young age. They witnessed drug abuse, alcohol induced violent rages and all manner of perversions. These children were hardened and streetwise far beyond their tender years.

In spite of this, we had many marvellous times and numerous people came to faith in the Lord Jesus Christ. One example of this was a family who lived just up the way from Grace's little shack. There were six children in the family and the father was an alcoholic. Moonshine was the order of the day. All sorts of ingredients were added in the hope of giving the drink a bigger kick. It was often made from rotting bread, fermenting pineapple skins and raisins. One could stay drunk on this home brew all day for just a few cents. When drunk, the man would become violent and beat the mother senseless and then start on the children. This usually happened on a Saturday night after a long session of imbibing.

One particular Saturday night when things got really out

of hand, the two older children escaped the shack and ran to Grace. She took them in for the night, gave them supper and a bed. The next morning was church and the children stayed for Sunday school. After that, they knew that if things got ruthless at home they could come to Grace and she would take them in. All six children eventually came to Sunday school and became regular attendees.

One Sunday morning when we arrived for the service, we were surprised to find Father, Mother and all six children in tow waiting for us. The father was a scrawny, wiry little man. He was irate and walked up to my huge, broad shouldered husband, poking him in the chest, demanding to know what we had done to his children. He claimed they now listened when their mother asked them to do something and they no longer annoyed him!

Gavin invited the man to come into the church and to listen for himself to the life-changing Gospel message. From then on the whole family started attending regularly. Over many months, one by one, the entire family came to faith in the Lord Jesus Christ. Everything changed for them. Although still incredibly poor, the violence and strife in the home was transformed into peace and stability. A changed man, the father stopped drinking and that money was used to put food on the table.

Some of the ladies in the shanty church started helping their neighbours with little acts of kindness. There was a blind man whose wife had left him due to his surliness and she had taken their daughter with her. He was incredibly bitter and angry with his lot. The ladies cared for him and then started bringing him along on a Sunday to the shanty church. After many months, he too made a life changing profession of faith in Jesus. The change in him was so drastic that, after a short while, his wife and child returned and they were a complete family once more.

We would often take our little dog along with us to the shanty church. To the average African shanty dweller, an animal had a job to do and was not viewed as a pet to be loved.

Our baby Whisper gets attention from needy children.

We saw many mangy dogs, starving, uncared for and unloved, chained near a shack and my heart would break for these animals. We used our beloved pet as an illustration for the children about how to care for God's creatures. We would love her and stroke her and allow the children to do the same.

On a particularly hot day, I could see that our little dog was in need of a drink of water. There was no running water so I had to walk quite a distance to the nearest communal tap. As I approached the muddy area surrounding the faucet, I saw a young child squatting on her haunches rocking something covered by a filthy rag in her arms. I bent down and asked her what it was. She told me it was her "baby". I asked if I may see her baby. She pulled the dirty cloth to one side and I was shocked to see just the leg of a doll!

This incident touched both Gavin and I so deeply that we decided to hold Christmas parties for the many impoverished children in the settlements where we served. This was the start of many Christmas's with huge parties for thousands of children. We would collect used toys from schools and churches and wash and repair them before redistributing them. For months beforehand, eyes would be fixed on to teddies faces, dresses sewn for dolls and wheels made for little cars. All would be lovingly restored to the best possible condition. What a blessing to see the absolute delight of a child receiving a doll or a toy car to call their very own for the first time!

We had teams of volunteers helping us since the task was huge. A blessed time was had by all. Teams of ladies would bake cupcakes and youth groups would bundle packs of sweets together. Children received not only a toy, but a hamper comprised of cakes, sweets and a cold drink. Added to this, we told them the gospel message, explaining that the reason we celebrate Christmas is to remember Jesus' birth.

We told them that by giving a gift we remember the gift He gave us of His life so that we may have life everlasting. We told stories, sang choruses, had mime artists and acted out plays.

Crowd control was important because things could turn chaotic in a flash. When this happened children would storm the people giving the gifts in order to grab what they could. We soon learned how to keep things in an orderly fashion.

Distributing Christmas gift hampers.

One year we decided to bus the children from one area, called Frog Marsh, to the mission station for their Christmas Party. This was a huge treat for them as most hadn't even been in a bus before. We loaded them in the vehicle and sang choruses all the way.

When the children arrived at the mission station, some of the volunteer ladies came out of the kitchen carrying large trays stacked high with cupcakes. The children stormed the women, grabbing as many cupcakes as their scrawny little arms could carry. Ignoring the icing that smeared their limbs

Gavin preparing for Christmas outreaches.

and tattered clothing, they totally destroyed the small cakes by squashing them to their pint-sized bodies. No amount of explaining that there was enough for everyone improved the situation.

Coming from a place of deprivation that neared starvation, they had no concept of what it was like for all to receive the same amount. This happened with the gifts we gave them as well. We had placed some children's playground equipment on the front lawn of the mission house, and as the children climbed the slides they would try and take their toys with them. Little girls would attempt to haul toy prams up the stairs of the slide and young boys would use the swing holding bikes or trikes. If a toy was left unattended for just a second it would be stolen by another child. To say we were totally shattered at the end of that day would be an understatement. It was one of the most difficult parties we ever gave.

At one point while still on the mission station, we decided to rear chickens to provide protein for malnourished people. Not being chicken farmers, we really weren't knowledgeable

Blind and destitute Elizabeth.

about the subject. However, the Lord blessed this endeavour and our chickens thrived. We gave live chickens to the folks in the shanties as this is what they preferred. It also relieved us of the burden of slaughtering them, which I was never able to cope with. As it was, I couldn't eat chicken for many years, even after we had stopped raising them.

Elizabeth was an old lady in the shanty town called Paddevlei. She was impoverished and had virtually nothing, and was a regular recipient of whatever aid we had. One day, we presented her with a huge fully grown chicken. She was delighted. When we arrived back a few days later we asked her if she had enjoyed her chicken. Elizabeth told us that no, her chicken was doing well, thank you. She was so lonely that she would rather go hungry and have some company.

She had tied the chicken by one leg with an old scrap of wire and we could see the blood supply to that leg had been cut off. We removed the wire and retied the chicken by the other leg with an old pair of pantyhose. That chicken survived for many months. The injured leg fell off and it happily hopped around on one leg, eating scraps of bread that was thrown to it. A few months later we arrived one day to find the chicken had finally made its way to the pot. Hunger won out in the end.

Chapter 2

Not All Was Plain Sailing

Not all was plain sailing. We had many tough times and not all who attended the church turned out as success stories—far from it.

One such story involves Phamandela, a little boy in our Sunday school who wormed his way into our hearts. He would walk about six kilometres from Wheiler's Farm to the mission station where we were situated. He would spend weekends with us and we treated him like our own.

Around this time we started skills training for some of the ladies from the shanty church in an effort to bring in some much needed funds for them. We experimented with various skills and found that chocolate moulding was the most successful. We made little chocolates for the local restaurants to give to their patrons on various special days such as Mother's or Father's Day. This was a great help in providing a small income for some of the ladies. I would drive to Wheiler's Farm in the morning, collect the ladies and take them to the mission station where we would work for the day before returning them in the evening. Our policy was always only to take ladies from the church.

One Sunday morning three ladies not known to us arrived at the shanty church asking to be taken into the skills program. We were hesitant until Phamandela informed us that one of the ladies was his older brothers' girlfriend. Since there was a connection to the church through Phamandela, we agreed for them to join. It was the worst possible decision that we could ever have made. They caused untold problems and much dissention between the other women folk.

Also, things started disappearing from the mission station. One day, when we discovered they were drunk, we called a halt to the fiasco. Returning to Wheiler's Farm that evening I informed them that they would no longer be taken into the skills program. They were very angry and threatened me, insisting that I would fetch them the following week. I went home and told Gavin that I had felt threatened, and he insisted that he would transport the ladies for a while. He believed that if they saw it was him fetching the other womenfolk, they would cause no further trouble. He was right and for about ten days he did all the transporting and there were no further problems.

I felt guilty because this was my responsibility and he was very busy. I started insisting that I be allowed to once again drive the ladies back and forth from the shanty town. He reluctantly agreed for me to do so. The very first day I arrived in Wheiler's Farm to fetch the ladies, someone must have noticed me. That evening, after dropping all the ladies at their various shanties, I was alone in the car and started down the dirt track which led to the main road. Suddenly, I saw three men in the middle of the road. As I got closer they did not moved out of the way, so I slowed down. It was only when I had stopped that I noticed all three men were pointing pistols at me. I slowly raised my hands and one of the men came to the window of the car pointing his gun at my head. I recognised him as Phamandela's older brother. He didn't have to say a word; his face was contorted with pure hatred and I knew he was going to kill me.

Before going into the ministry, Gavin had been a detective dealing with robberies and murder. He always told me that if I ever found myself in a threatening situation, to do something unexpected, as this gives one a chance of escape. Unfortunately, I am not a quick thinker and it is not in my nature to act in this way, therefore I know that our faithful Lord was totally in control.

With the gun against my temple, I suddenly lowered my upper body as far as the steering wheel would allow and hit the accelerator as hard as I could. The car spun off crazily as I couldn't see where I was going, but I knew that the road ahead was fairly straight. I have no idea what happened to the other two gangsters in the road since my head was down.

Phamandela's brother was so intent on killing me that, as I pulled off, he lowered the gun and fired anyway. The bullet hit the locking mechanism of the car door, deflected downward, entered my right thigh, travelled through my leg and exited near the inside of my knee. The bullet buried itself in the floor of the passenger side of the car.

As it was my right leg, I could still change gears with my left foot and keep my right foot on the petrol pedal. I managed to drive back to the mission station on pure adrenalin! When I arrived at the gate, sitting in the blood soaked driver's seat, I found that I couldn't get out of the car. I placed my hand on the hooter and kept it there until Gavin came running out. When I saw him, I relaxed knowing he would take care of me. I went into shock and don't remember much after that.

Gavin raced with me to the nearest hospital where I underwent surgery to repair the damage done to my leg. The doctor spoke to me afterwards and said he had never seen a bullet travel the length of the thigh in such a manner without nicking the main artery. He said that if it had, I would have bled to death within minutes. What a faithful God we serve! I was lost in awe and wonder at this bit of information and prayed, "Oh dear Lord, why did you spare my life?" These words popped into my mind: "Because I have work for you to do!" One may say that it was the medication talking, but I firmly believe my Father answered my question that night.

The police were called because the hospital was required to report all gunshot wounds. They took a statement and informed us that the special branch would check for finger prints and dig the bullet out of the car.

After my stay in hospital, I was ready to come home and the police had still not contacted Gavin regarding the fingerprints or the bullet which was still lodged in the floor of the car. He wanted to clean it of all the blood so as not to traumatise me any further.

He called the police station to find out when they would

be coming, only to discover that there was no docket number and therefore no case. It had all disappeared. It was common practise in those days for criminals to bribe certain officials to "loose" a docket number which then made the case disappear.

There was never any follow-up on this incident; no one was ever prosecuted for the attempted murder, even though we knew who the perpetrators were and the motive. I was very angry about the whole episode and cried out to God, "Lord, where is your justice in all of this?" I was reminded of the Bible verse that says, "Vengeance is mine, I will repay says the Lord" (Romans 12:19 New American Standard Bible). I was eventually able to accept that scripture and found peace and forgiveness in my heart towards those three men. It took time, and three years of panic attacks, to finally overcome that incident, God is good and He helped me every step of the way.

We later learned that Phamandela's older brother had been shot and killed during another attempted carjacking. The driver of the vehicle had a concealed weapon, and after being shot by Phamandela's brother, pulled it out and shot him dead.

The second thug had been caught raping a young girl in one of the shanty towns. Police seldom ventured into these areas and so the locals began a "Kangaroo Court" system which was a form of civic law enforcement. The Kangaroo Court administered justice to the rapist by beating him so badly that he was confined to a wheelchair.

The third perpetrator involved in my attempted murder was caught in a shoot-out with police after a bank robbery.

His throat was shot away and he has lost the power of speech. The last we heard of this man, he was still in prison.

An important principal in the Bible was played out through all of this—"You live by the sword, you die by the sword". As Jesus said, "Put your sword back into its place. For all who take the sword will perish by the sword." (Matthew 26:52 English Standard Version). We have seen much evidence of this over the years. Violence begets violence and peace can be restored only when a heart is changed by God's love.

Needless to say, some expected us then to withdraw from the work. We were told that we would never go back and it was implied that somehow this was my own fault. We were also criticized. People said that we had probably "walked out from under the protection of God's umbrella" or that we were being punished for some secret sin in our lives. We knew that this was not the case.

We live in a fallen world and the Lord doesn't always protect His people from the dangers in it. We have seen far too many missionaries killed or injured while serving in the field. God wants us to face the future with faith. On the day of my release from hospital, Gavin took me straight back into Wheiler's Farm, to the very spot of the shooting. He explained that it was like riding a bicycle. When one falls off the bike, one needs to get back up straight away. My heart was pounding, my throat was dry, my palms were sweaty, but in retrospect it was the best possible thing to do. We went back to that work immediately, and that spoke volumes to the inhabitants. They could see that we were seriously committed to the work and to them.

There have been many incidents of the Lord's protection in our lives. For example, we were in the shanty town of Paddevlei feeding the local children and were just about to leave when one of the young boys, Thabang, came running up to us. He told us there were some Mozambican gangsters with guns lying in wait for us. They were planning to hijack our vehicle.

We turned in the opposite direction and sped away as fast as we could. Thabang put his own life in danger that day, for if the gangsters had discovered he was the one who had warned us, his life would have been worth nothing.

Thabang grew into a lovely young man but was never able to escape the confines of his poverty. He married at a very young age and had a son in a short space of time. Thabang phoned us one day asking for extra aid. He told us that his wife was so malnourished that she could no longer produce breast milk and their child was going hungry. We were not aware of this dire situation since Thabang had not mentioned it before. We hastily gathered supplies together—baby formula, baby clothes and groceries for Thabang and his wife.

The morning we were due to deliver the supplies, we received a telephone call from Thabang's distraught mother. She informed us that on the previous evening, while Thabang was on his way back to his little shack, he tripped over an illegal electrical connection and was electrocuted and killed.

The family could not afford a funeral and we were left to pay for the burial of this lovely young man. Within six months of this tragedy, Thabang's wife left their young son and went off with another man. Thabang's mother, a woman well advanced in years, was left to care for the little boy. She had no means of her own and to this day we support her so she can bring up the child.

Granny Patricia with Thabangs' child.

We have had many burglaries over the years. Some have been more traumatic than others, but we have never been harmed in any way during these times, as is the case with so many other folks in South Africa. We have heard the most blood chilling tales of horrendous torture, murder and rape. Thankfully, most of the burglaries we experienced have been while we were away from our residence.

For example, one evening when we arrived home, we noticed some movement in the dark shadows and that my car, which had been parked in the open garage, had been pushed out into the driveway. When we entered the house we discovered many of our belongings had been stolen. We called the police and they warned us it was probably a pre-liminary burglary. If they were true to their usual modus operandi, the thieves would be back in a few days to finish off what they had started.

A minister friend of ours strongly urged Gavin to arm him-self, just for a short while, for our own protection. This was not something we had ever done before, but under the circumstanc-es, Gavin accepted the rifle the minister was offering on loan.

Sure enough, barely a week later, in the early hours one morning, we heard the dogs barking. Since we were hyper-vigilant knowing what was likely to occur, we immediately got out of bed and in the darkness peered through the windows. We couldn't see much through the inky blackness of the night, but we could see movement of sorts. Thinking it might be the neighbours' horses, we were not sure what to do. Our wooden front door had a middle glass panel which opened on a hinge. Gavin opened this panel and I sat on the floor in front of it. Gavin trained the rifle through the door, resting the barrel on my shoulder. We stayed like that until the sun peeked over the horizon. Later that day we learned that a group of burglars had indeed come back, but had gone to our neighbours instead. Thankfully, they survived the attack.

Others have not been so fortunate. Just before we moved from the last mission station we were on, we had seventeen of our neighbours attacked and murdered in a twelve month pe-riod. The last was a lovely old German couple who lived across the road from us. The murderers gained access by removing ceiling tiles. They hacked the couple to death before robbing the home.

The last straw was when a fellow worker living just down the road from us was ambushed as she was returning from work one evening. Rose and her daughter were both gang raped and severely beaten. This was the catalyst which caused our home church to counsel us to move away from the area before we became a statistic. This we did, moving to Pretoria, into a more traditional suburb and into a gated complex where the conditions were considered to be much safer. We had not been in our new home long before we were burgled once again. All our doors were damaged by forced entry and the burglar lit matches and threw them, still burning, on the carpets. The feeling of being invaded is difficult to describe and the keen loss of security and safety is dreadful.

We then undertook some security measures and installed a burglar alarm, security bars and gates. Not long after that incident, I awoke one morning to find the bedroom window, which happens to be right next to my head when I'm asleep, had been forced open. When investigating outside, we discovered a huge knife lying on the ground outside the window. We can only surmise that the burglar had been interrupted in his awful crime and we had been spared another horrendous attack.

The gang culture is widespread. Because the children in these areas are so streetwise, they tend to be tough. Once, a group of five to six year-olds were playing in Wheiler's Farm, when an altercation broke out amongst them. One child was held down by the others who then tried to slit his throat using a blunt knife. Thankfully one of our co-workers, who helped out in a makeshift clinic nearby, happened to be passing by and rescued the child. There was a nasty cut on the child's neck only inches from the artery.

The gang culture also had a big influence on young children. There were two boys in our Sunday school who were life-long friends. Wilson heard that Abel had acquired a knife and asked to have a look at it. Abel replied that if he showed Wilson the knife he would have to use it on him. Wilson did not take this threat seriously and insisted, until eventually Abel pulled out the knife and plunged it into Wilson's young chest, killing him instantly.

The witch doctors were often a real menace. They did not appreciate our presence and saw us as a threat. We counselled our folks not to seek out the witch doctor, but to go instead to Jesus with their problems and daily needs.

A witch doctors' wife started coming to the shanty church in Wheiler's Farm, and after a while she made a profession of faith in the Lord Jesus Christ. Her husband was furious and vowed to do us harm. One night, our friend Grace was awakened by the witch doctor and some of his cohorts, who were trying to break into her little shack. They shouted that they were going to kill her because of her witness for Christ. Grace prayed. Being elderly and alone, she was no match for a group of tough, strong men. The only piece of furniture of any substance in Grace's home was a big old filing cabinet where she stored her personal belongings. The witch doctor chose that very spot in the wall to break in! He couldn't get through the wall because the filing cabinet was in the way. God protected Grace that night!

One evening as Gavin was coming from another shanty

town, he was confronted by a gun-toting thug. The villain walked over to the window intending to hijack our vehicle when a look of recognition came across his face. He looked at Gavin and said, "I know you!" Months earlier, we had taken this man in and allowed him to stay in one of the outbuildings on the mission station for a short time. After a pause, the man shouted at Gavin, "Go!" He then pointed the gun at him and said, "Pastor, we are now even. Next time I shoot!"

Gavin first started working in a place called Kliptown and he preached his very first sermon there. A number of people were converted and a small church was planted. There was nowhere for the church to meet—the only place offered to us

Earliest evangelistic outreach.

was the backyard of a brothel. For many months we met in this filthy yard, packed full of all sorts of rubbish. Yet, we had wonderful times of worship amidst the stench and the muck and ignored the goings-on inside the house in front of us.

There were two sisters who came to faith in Jesus round this time. Kate and Michelle changed and wanted to live Godly lives. We were able to help them move into a small dwelling in a neighbouring area. One of the little boys in that family was snatched by some local gangsters and forced through a tiny window of a house. They made him open the front door from

Kate, Josephs' Aunt.

the inside so they could rob the house. When finally released, he ran home to tell his mother what happened. She promptly took him to the police station where they took a statement. When the gangsters heard about this they made it known that they wanted the child dead.

We took little Joseph into our home for a time for his own protection. He caused us untold problems as he did not seem to grasp the meaning of the word, "NO". We would tell him not to do something and he would blatantly look you in the eye and do whatever it was that you had asked him not to do. This went on for many months until eventually the storm seemed to have passed and Joseph's mother wanted him home again.

By this time, Joseph had gotten used to the luxuries of electricity, running water and a bathroom. He didn't want to go back! We had to force him, as it was his mother's right to have him under her care. We would take him home only to

Joseph before he contracted HIV/AIDS.

have him run away within a few hours and return to us. Sometimes he would arrive at the mission station in the middle of the night and we would have to get into our car and return him immediately to his mother. It was a difficult time and Joseph never fully grasped the meaning of the word "NO". He came to Sunday school every week and grew into a young man. Although he knew the gospel message, we never heard him make a profession of faith, and at the age of sixteen he was convicted of rape. He was sent to a juvenile correctional facility for twelve months.

Upon his release he moved away from the area, but we still kept in touch with him in the hope of making a difference in his life. Later, we heard that he shot a security guard and was jailed for that offence. Joseph is today a young man in his late 20's, dying of AIDS, in a wheelchair with his leg amputated. Our hearts break for a wasted life and a continued rejection of the saving knowledge of Christ. We are still in contact with Joseph and still lift him in prayer. It is never too late to come to Jesus!

Chapter 3

Beginning of the Rural Work

We were staying on a small holding just south of the city of Johannesburg and had gained a reputation for helping those in need. Folks came knocking on our door seeking assistance with one necessity or another at all times of the day or night. We often took people in, giving them a place to stay for a short period of time. Most often, the greatest need was for food. We also had an endless stream of urchins asking for cake! We used to receive huge donations of individually wrapped, delicious small cakes, which we would give to the children. They really enjoyed them. They could not afford even any small luxury, so it was a huge treat for them.

Unfortunately, this area was a stronghold of the right-wing political party of the Afrikaners, and they were not kindly disposed to what we were doing. A couple of men arrived one day while we were out. They attacked and beat up some of the young people we had temporarily living in a number of the outbuildings. The young people were given a message for us— we were to move! We did not want to be intimidated, so decided to ignore the incident and carried on as normal. About three months later a pickup van arrived one afternoon with a group of these Afrikaner men on the back. The burley group of men screamed, "Get out! Be gone with you! You will leave now if you know what's good for you! You are not wanted here!"

"What now Lord? Where to from here?" we silently cried. Where were we to go? We had no idea.

It was a frightening situation. I phoned the police while Gavin was trying to reason with them, only to be told that they could not intervene until violence had been perpetrated. We prayed and felt the Lord leading us to quietly pack our things and go. "A quiet answer turns away wrath", the Bible says, and although it was difficult for us to leave, we knew we had to do that.

We had nowhere to go and couldn't afford to pay someone to move us either. Gavin phoned a friend who kindly lent us his open back pickup truck, and then he went house hunting. In the meantime, I took large refuse bags and went to every cupboard and just threw the contents into these bags.

Gavin eventually found a lady whose husband was away on a business trip, and who owned a house intended for rental. It wasn't quite finished and ready to go on the market yet; it had no electricity, no running water and bare cement floors. We were desperate and Gavin pleaded with her to allow us to stay there. She finally agreed and said we could move in right away. She said her husband would be back from his trip in four days and we could discuss terms and conditions with him.

We were relieved to have a place to move to, and Gavin and I then started the laborious task of carting out the furniture, piece by piece, from the house and loading it onto the pickup. It took all night since it was just the two of us, and the small pickup couldn't take more than one piece of furniture at a time.

By the next morning, totally exhausted, we had all the furniture moved, and a mountain of unmarked black refuse bags in the centre of the lounge filled with the rest of our belongings. It took three days of sorting to finally locate everything and get some semblance of normality back into our lives. We would have to fetch large barrels of water from a nearby petrol filling station and we used a small gas cooker to prepare food by candlelight. Being city born and bred, this was difficult for us and we were thrown far outside our comfort zone.

Still exhausted after a stressful and physically demanding five days, we then had to visit the businessman to come to some kind of agreement regarding rent. We were greeted affably, and then asked to explain our situation. When we mentioned that we were Christians, the whole mood suddenly changed. The businessman demanded that we leave his property immediately. He told us he had previously rented another property to some "so-called Christian organisation". They did not pay him for months and then disappeared in the middle of the night. We pleaded with him to allow us to stay long enough to find another property. He reluctantly gave us until the end of that month—just a little short of three weeks—to vacate the premises.

"Lord, oh Lord", I cried, "What is going on?" We felt like refugees, no one wanting us on their door step—just settling in one place before being forced to move on to the next. Once again we found ourselves having to pack up and move. Gavin eventually found a lovely little home to rent and we moved before the end of that month.

At the same time, we began to hear rumours of incredible suffering of Mozambican refugees who had fled their native country due to the civil war there, and had crossed the border into South Africa. We had no peace upon hearing this, and feeling like refugees ourselves, could empathise with what they were going through. Ah—the goodness of our Lord! He allowed us to experience the hardships to teach us what it feels like to have to leave your home in a hurry and live under difficult circumstances.

We loaded our vehicle with what supplies we could procure and headed to the northeast of our country. What we found was horrific and distressing. In this particular African culture, the man, who is the head of the household, eats first. Being polygamists, they have any number of wives. Since African men generally like their women rather plump, they made sure that the wives got whatever food was left. Only scraps were passed to the children. We find this abhorrent in our western culture, but to them it is the norm.

The system of Labola, which is something akin to paying a dowry, is still widely practised. When pressed about the issue of children going hungry, eventually one man told us that it is easier to have another child than it is to buy another wife!

Through some other missionaries working in the area, we set up a long distance feeding scheme for the children, which continued until the troubles ended and most of the refugees were repatriated.

While involved in this project, neighbouring villages heard about what we were doing and came asking us to help them also. When this work originally began, Gavin had prayed to

Needy children in rags.

the Lord saying that he would never say no to anyone in need, if the Lord would graciously provide. We watched in amazement as food was delivered to the Mission base from many different places and from the most unexpected of sources.

We had plenty and were able to provide for all those seeking assistance. We started going into the neighbouring villages with food and aid of various kinds. This led to the planting of churches which are still in existence today.

A few months after being forced off the property by the Afrikaner men, Gavin encountered the ringleader of that group in a shop. Gavin was surprised when this man came over and started to chat to him. He told Gavin that our quiet and gentle attitude of forgiveness, and moving in such a hurry, had left him with a guilty conscience and no peace. Later, he began attending a church and was gloriously converted. He asked Gavin for forgiveness and they were wonderfully reconciled that day.

During this period we decided to take a two-day break and visit The Kruger National Park. It is South Africa's largest game park, where the animals roam freely as they have since time immortal. Being wildlife enthusiasts, this was a real treat for us and we stayed in a rest camp within the park.

The rules of the park are strictly observed because of the dangers of the wild animals to humans. The camps are surrounded by electrified fences, and the gates to the camps are opened and closed at certain times. Failure to adhere to these times results in a hefty fine being issued. Timing was a consideration when Gavin wanted to take me to see a Fever tree forest in the north of the park. These trees are fascinating as the bark is of a bright lime green colour and the trees look as though they have a fever. We checked the distance we needed to travel and allowed ourselves plenty of time to enjoy the day and arrive back safely in the camp before the gates closed for the night. We had a lovely day out, enjoying the marvels of God's beautiful creation. Zebra, Impala, Warthogs and Giraffes were in abundance and Elephants too. Lions, Cheetahs and Rhinos more scarce, but we did get glimpses of them as well.

We were on our way back to the camp when my darling husband suddenly took a wrong turn and started heading in the opposite direction! Being totally confused, I asked him what he thought he was doing, only to be told that he was heading for the exit gate. Outside of the park at that particular exit gate, in those days, was nothing but wild expanse and a couple of little huts dotted in amongst the bush. Our luggage was still at the rest camp and there was simply not enough time to go to the exit gate and get back to the camp before the gates closed. Gavin insisted that he felt led by the Lord to go to the exit gate, but for what purpose he did not know. I was furious with him, not understanding this kind of leading. It was my first experience of my husband's extraordinary faith, but certainly not the last!

We drove in tense, stony silence for a while until eventually we saw the exit gate looming ahead. There was one solitary employee manning the gate. He stood by the exit, expecting us to stop and hand him our papers to be stamped, allowing us to leave the park with no return. This, we obviously did not want to do, so Gavin pulled over to the side of the road and got out of the car.

The gate keeper, in confusion, came over to chat to Gavin and find out what we were doing. Since we had no idea why we were there, Gavin started making small talk with the man.

As the conversation started to flow, this man, whose name was Strike Madeba, revealed that he used to be the pastor of a church. Regrettably, the church was so impoverished that they couldn't support him and he was forced to seek employment. The only work he could find was manning this gate in the remotest part of our country. He was hardly seeing people, let alone Christians, and felt he was dying inside spiritually. He had prayed that morning asking the Lord to bring someone across his path who would pray with him.

What a joy and blessing to be able to spend time with this wonderful man just praying and worshipping our God! I was humbled by this experience and never again doubted my husband's leading. It was a sharp learning curve for me to adjust to the idea of walking by faith and not by sight.

After a time in prayer and fellowship with Strike, we needed to head back to the rest camp where we were staying for the night. We knew we would never make it before the camp gates closed and were not sure what to do. This was in the days before mobile phones and we couldn't phone ahead and explain. Strike told us to go and to drive at the speed limit. He said that he would pray, as would we.

When we finally arrived at the rest camp, we were over an hour late, but to our utter amazement the camp gates were still open. We worked in the park with the employees there for many years after this incident and the gates were never left open after closing time again, that we knew of. As we drove through the gates, a game ranger riding on a bicycle came up behind us and closed the gates. What a mighty God we serve. He takes care of even the tiniest details.

This was the beginning of a wonderful friendship with Strike that lasted many years. The fruit of Gavin's obedience that day had far reaching consequences. We visited Strike often, supplying him with books to keep him from being discouraged. Strike went on to help us plant a small church in a local village called Tsikuyu, 30 kilometres from the most northerly gate of the park. We started the church with twelve members and a Pastor. The church grew and flourished and after nurturing it for a number of years, we, together with the members of that church, planted a second one in a nearby village named Bant Mutale. That church flourished as well. After more years passed, those two churches, without our aid, went on to plant a third church in the village of Dohvo where all three congregations now meet. The combined church has over five hundred members and a Sunday school of hundreds. The locals are bussed in on the back of open lorries as there is no public transport in the vicinity. The trucks start heading out at seven in the morning to fetch people for a service that starts at ten thirty. Wonderful work is being done by those three churches out in the bush, and all through one man being obedient to the still small voice in his heart.

In the early stages of the third church being established, the Pastor, Leonard Baizie, who used to be a builder before becoming the Pastor, felt led to construct a church building. We agreed to help fund the project but were surprised at the magnitude of the structure. We felt that people looking in on this project must have thought of us like the people did when Noah built an ark with no water for miles. Here we were, building a massive church building with a mere handful of people.

We started ordering cement, sand, stone and bricks from the nearest building supplier which was about two hundred kilometres away. It cost huge amounts of money in delivery charges, and when eventually the cost rose to sixty per cent of the value of the bricks, we knew that this could not continue.

It was decided that the people in the church should help make their own bricks. Forty-two thousand bricks were made to complete the half-built church.

Today, the church stands proud and tall, all but the finishing touches to be added. A testimony to one man's obedience

The congregation in the Dovho Church.

and another man's vision; the church and its members are seeking to serve the needy and lost, and reaching folks with the love of a faithful awesome God. As mentioned earlier, this church presently has approximately five hundred adults attending, along with a couple hundred children.

Strike was eventually transferred from that remote gate to

the biggest rest camp in the park. There he headed up a training program for park employees. He also started a Bible College in the nearest African town, which was Bushbuck Ridge.

Strike did wonderful work for the Lord and he was very dear to us. When his mother passed away he had to catch an African taxi, which is a small minibus, back home to attend the funeral. While waiting on the side of the road, another bus came by, lost control and ploughed into him, killing him instantly. We were saddened to have Strike no longer with us, but know his work on earth was obviously at an end and his legacy lives on through the planted churches and the Bible school.

Strike Madeba, far left with Gavin.

The easiest and safest way to reach remote rural villages was to cut through the northern tip of The Kruger National Park. We saw numerous wild animals on our travels and had many encounters with them. One memorable incident was when we came around a bend in the road while pulling a trailer. It was a dirt road and the car was throwing up a lot of dust. Suddenly, we saw a huge bull elephant right in the middle of the road, eating leaves off of a tree. He got a terrible fright as we rounded the bend and Gavin slammed on the brakes. The dust bellowed up around the car making the elephant even angrier. One always knows when an elephant is about to charge because the warning signs are very clear. They sway their huge heads from side to side and transfer weight from one large foot to the other; they lift their trunks and trumpet—then charge! This bull elephant was displaying all of these warning signs and we knew we needed to get out of there fast.

Unfortunately, we were on a single dirt track road, and with a trailer on the back it was difficult to turn around. There was dense bush on both sides of the road making our situation even more impossible. We started praying out loud, "Lord, help us!" Then Gavin said to me "Quick—open the windows." This we did, and playing on the stereo in the car, was the "Shotts and Dykehead" Scottish Pipe band. Gavin turned the music up full blast. That poor old elephant had never heard such a strange sound. He put his tail between his legs and went scurrying away into the bush. How grateful we were for pipe band music that day. Not only did it put terrible fear into Scottish enemies on the battlefield, but it put fear into a raging elephant as well.

One year it was unseasonably wet and most of the rivers in the park had burst their banks. Many of the roads were flooded and we had to try and find an alternate route home. We were still inside the park and the only way out involved crossing a small stream using the car. One of the rules in the park, which is strictly enforced, is that of staying in your vehicle at all times. Under no circumstances may you get out of your car unless in a protected area.

We decided to try to cross the stream as we needed to get home and couldn't afford to pay for another night's accommodation in the park. We managed half way across before the vehicle became lodged on some rocks and wouldn't budge. We were stuck in the middle of the stream and couldn't move.

There was no signal for mobile phones in this area back then, so we could not call for help. After some minutes, another vehicle came along also wanting to cross at the same point. After an hour or so there were about four vehicles on the banks of this stream, all of us not knowing what to do. We prayed. Our prayers were answered when a game ranger just happened to drive by in a Jeep. He had a rifle with him and commandeered the men in the other vehicles to wade into the stream and pick our car up off the rocks while he looked out for wild animals. We were relieved to get out of that stream. It was only then the game ranger pointed out fresh lion spoor in the sand indicating that a lion was nearby.

On another trip we were told that three lions had escaped from The Kruger National Park and were killing the local villagers' cattle. Due to heavy rains, the road we usually traversed had washed away and once again we were forced to detour on a road which led us into the back and beyond of nowhere.

We drove for hours on nothing more than a single gravel track. Our growing concern was quickly becoming something akin to panic. We had not seen a village, huts, people or cattle for miles and it was getting late in the evening. Around midnight we finally came to a place where the dirt track simply disappeared. In its place was a vast stretch of thick slushy mud and one could see tyre imprints where cars and trucks had become stuck. The evidence of their struggles was firmly imprinted in the sludge.

I told Gavin that we would have to turn around and go back along the road we had struggled upon for so many hours. "What!" he cried, "no way!" We sat in tense silence for a few moments and then both broke out in spontaneous prayer. No sooner had we finished praying when we saw shadowy movement breaking through the darkness. Was it the lions, I wondered? But then, to our utter astonishment, a row of white teeth materialised in front of us. Africans in this part of our land are extremely dark and so in the pitch darkness we couldn't see them except for their beautiful smiles! There before us stood three young mothers with babies tied on their backs. We never did find out what these precious young women and their children were doing out in the middle of the night.

Their English was extremely poor and we couldn't speak Venda. With eleven official languages in our country it was easiest for us to use an interpreter when Gavin was preaching. Through a lot of frantic hand gesturing, they indicated to us not to go any further. We agreed and said we could see the road was not passable. They then motioned for us to follow them. We turned the vehicle around and the three mothers ran in front of the car, in the reflected lights shining from the headlamps.

We came to a place in the "road" where the ladies stopped and pushed back some bushes to reveal a tiny footpath. They pointed us on to the path, demonstrating we should drive there instead. We thanked them profusely and wanted to give them something for their kindness, but before we were able to do that, they disappeared. It was so dark that we jokingly said all they needed to do to vanish was to close their mouths and their beautiful white teeth would disappear.

Gavin preaching in the Dovho Church.

They became rescuing angels to us that night, and we were so very grateful. We were able to drive on the footpath for a few kilometres before joining up once again with the original dirt track. We reached our home the next morning and were utterly spent by the experience.

We still regularly travel the five hundred plus kilometres

to see the folks in these rural churches. They love us as we love them. They call us their grandparents and it's an honour and a joy to be that to them.

While still living on the mission station in Johannesburg, we befriended the pastor of a shanty church very near to where we were living. Klass was the assistant in the local butchery, who, over weekends, became the Pastor of the shanty church just behind the butchery.

The shanty church in Khakhala.

We were able to assist him and his congregation. When he retired, he moved back to his ancestral home, which was in the village of Khakhala in the region of Giyani. As this was also far out in the bush, in the northern regions of our country, it was included into our rural mission fields.

Klass and his wife, Violet, now both well advanced in years, continue to faithfully proclaim God's word in that village. They grow peanuts and maize behind their small home which they freely share with all in need. We still supply vital aid to them in terms of clothing, food, Bibles, financial support and refreshments which are given to the children before Sunday school.

Many of our rural children did not travel far beyond their own villages. Electricity was not available in most of these areas, and the folks were economically deprived as a result. There were no televisions, iPads or computers in the homes. When we told the children the stories of Noah and the ark or Jonah and the big fish, some had difficulty grasping the concept of the ocean as they had never travelled to the seaside.

Joy at receiving Illustrated childrens' Bibles.

We decided to buy each child in all of our Sunday schools a beautifully illustrated children's Bible. Each story in the Bible had a delightful picture and the children could read the story for themselves. What joy and delight when these Bibles were given out! In some cases it was the only book these children ever owned.

Chapter 4

Travelling Further Afield

In December of 1992, my father passed away and my sister and mother relocated from the city of Johannesburg to the Cape Province. Fish Hoek is a town approximately 1,500 hundred kilometres from where we live in the city of Pretoria. We started to visit my family once a year, undertaking the journey by car. It took two days of travel, and we slept over approximately half way.

On the journey we encountered many people living by the roadside, under bushes or in caves. The coloured folks in the Karoo (a semi-desert region of South Africa), many of them descendants of the Koi San and Hottentot peoples of our land, live in extreme poverty. We were blessed to give them a measure of relief in terms of food and financial aid.

Although in some countries, the term "coloured" is not politically correct to use, it is widely used and accepted in South Africa. Coloured folks are people of mixed ancestry making them neither Black nor European. Their language and culture is the same as the Afrikaans people of our land. Coloured folk make up the majority of the population in the Cape Province.

It was a delight to see the gratitude and shock on some of their faces when presented with their gifts. How true the words, "It is more blessed to give than to receive." We have seen this time and time again over the many years that we have been doing this work. We encountered some children too, with whom we were able to bless with some small gifts and pocket money.

Urchins begging outside a fast food outlet.

We started to use these trips for outreach purposes, especially to children and old folks. I will never forget encountering some street children begging outside a local fast food outlet. We bought them some food and while chatting to them enquired after their parents. One child said his mother was dead. When asked about his father, he told us that his father was in prison for killing his mother. This is just one example of the many children who fell through the cracks in our social system, which continues to be under extreme pressure even today.

Alcoholism and drug abuse continues to be a huge curse on our nation. One child told us that most of the money that came into his home was spent on alcohol and he and his siblings had to beg for food. This was by no means an isolated case. So this outreach has become a biannual event and takes us across the Cape Province and lasts for approximately six weeks at a time.

Many old folks across our land find themselves in dire straits. Many travelled to South Africa in their early years to work on the gold mines and, for one reason or another, did not return to their homelands. Never being registered in

Gavin giving a bucket of groceries to a destitute old man.

South Africa as immigrants, they did not qualify for the meagre state pension in their old age.

This left many of them eking out an existence, living from hand-to-mouth on a daily basis. Our home church helped us to buy plastic buckets and the congregation filled them with groceries. They donated tea, coffee, sugar, maize meal, tins of fish and meat, beans, jam, peanut butter, biscuits and sweets. The bucket was a useful commodity and once emptied of the contents, it could be used to store water, wash in or even sat upon!

We also supplied the old folks with blankets for the cold winter nights. South Africa has very little cloud cover most

Giving a cup of cold water in the name of the Lord.

days, and as soon as the sun sets the heat dissipates and it becomes extremely cold.

When talking to these old folks one would get a sense of

their feelings of despair and hopelessness. They felt that they had been tossed aside by society and left to rot like a piece of garbage. After spending some time with them, and telling them about a heavenly Father who loves them and cares for them, we had a sense that some of the God-given dignity that is within all of us, had been restored. This ministry continues to the present day.

Once in the Cape, we started to see huge needs all around us. We became involved with a small day care centre run by two volunteer ladies. The adults who sent their children to this

Children sleeping on the floor at Tiny Tots Day Care Centre.

day care centre worked mainly on the neighbouring farms as fruit pickers. This being seasonal work, they struggled the rest of the year to find some sort of employment just to get by.

The fruit farm salaries were so low that the people battled

to survive. For this reason, the parents were not able to afford to send their children to professional day care centres and this voluntary nursery school was all that was available to them. The centre was in dire need. There was no electricity, the children were sleeping on the floor, eating out of used margarine tubs and generally the place was short of everything a day care centre would need. There were very few toys or books and no tables or chairs.

Over the years we have been privileged to supply electricity, chairs, tables, books, toys, eating utensils, food, clothing, mattresses, blankets and fans for the hot summer months. We are regular visitors and Gavin is fondly referred to as "Opie", which is a term of endearment for a grandfather.

In the 1850's Gavin's great grandfather left Dundee, Scotland and travelled to South Africa with the London Mission Society. He settled in the town of Graaf Reinet and was good friends with another famous missionary, Dr Andrew Murray, who also lived and worked in the same town.

Quinton Campbell was a school teacher and was involved in educating the Coloured children in Graaf Reinet and surrounding areas, which at that time, was frowned upon. Because of the tie with the town of Graaf Reinet and Quinton Campbell, we felt a need to get involved in the area, even though it was about a thousand kilometres from our home base. Gavin felt that by ministering to the Coloured folks in Graaf Reinet, he could be helping the descendants of those with whom his great grandfather had worked with all those years ago.

We started by supporting the local church (which continues today) in the needy township just outside of the town. We supplied the Pastor with Afrikaans Bibles to give to those in his congregation who could not afford one. The Pastor's wife would get up at three am on a Sunday morning to cook a meal for the Sunday school children. This was often the only hot meal the children would receive all week.

After a while, some Xhosa people started attending the church. The Xhosa people are one of the ethnic black tribes

Gavin with Pastor and Mrs Tom receiving a case of Bibles.

residing in South Africa. Pastor Tom now had to use an interpreter, as he would preach in Afrikaans and the interpreter would then preach in Xhosa. We subsequently had to provide Xhosa Bibles for those folks.

South Africa's eleven official languages can be a logistical nightmare. Thankfully, Gospel tracts are available in all eleven languages and we used them widely. We distribute around fifteen thousand tracts each year. The only reason why we know the figure is simply because we have to order them.

In every area we went, we made sure that we had tracts in the local languages with us to distribute. Slowly, as schools become better equipped, children are learning to read, especially in their own language. We would take sweets for the children

Children in the Cape with our hampers and tracts.

and hand out a sweet with a tract. The children, being so needy, never refused the sweet or the tract and we would witness children hunkering down on their haunches on the roadside reading the tract. How we prayed, that the Lord would plant seeds in little hearts that would grow and take root!

While in the Cape each year, we tried to take a week or two off as a holiday period. This almost never happened. We were too aware of the needs around us and could not turn a blind eye to the suffering we witnessed.

We often stayed in a caravan park in the town of Knysna which was surrounded by a wire fence. People would walk past the fence and ask for assistance from those inside. We could never ignore these people and often after providing food and financial assistance, we would spend time telling them about Jesus. With regularity we heard heart breaking stories of lives in pieces and of shattered dreams, of lives filled with struggles and deprivation. Although we couldn't solve their problems we were able to give them hope in Christ Jesus.

Just outside of the caravan park there was a designated area, where casual day labourers would gather waiting for work. Often these men would sit there all day in the hope that someone would offer them a job.

One evening around 6 pm, there were still some men milling around. They told us that they didn't want to go home as they had nothing to take back for their wives and children to eat. We were saddened by these stories and did whatever we were able to bring a measure of relief.

Outside of the town of Knysna, there is a large shanty settlement. We would go in there distributing sweets and tracts to the children as well as food hampers and money to the old folks.

On one particular trip, we encountered a very old man walking alongside the road. We stopped and offered him a lift. While driving to the shanty settlement where he was headed, he told us that he had been renting a small dwelling but was unable to pay the rent the previous month. He and his family had been locked out of their home and were sleeping in the outside toilet.

We saw so much of this kind of poverty and it broke our hearts. I had to make sure that I looked at each individual case and knew that we had made a difference in that person's life. One must be able to focus on individuals or problems become overwhelming.

In looking at each individual case, I would be reminded of the story of the star fish. It went something like this:

A young boy was walking along a beach, upon which hundreds of starfish had been washed ashore. He kept bending down, picking up one after the next and throwing them back into the sea.

A man was watching the boy and eventually called out to him to stop. "You can't possibly help them all, just give it up!" he cried.

The boy stopped for a moment, then bent down picked up one starfish and through it back into the ocean.

Looking up at the man, he answered, "To that ONE, I have made a difference!"

This is the principal by which I look at the many hundreds of folks that we have helped.

Chapter 5

Kwa Zulu Natal

Just after I was shot, back in the late 1990's, a friend in our home church offered us the use of her holiday cottage in the town of Ramsgate on the Natal south coast. It was an opportunity for me to heal both physically and emotionally.

While there, we befriended the employee who looked after the property in the owners' absence. Stefans lived in a little outside room at the back of the house, but had a home in the large Zulu settlement of Izingolweni. Stefans was a lovely Christian man who would hold church services in the garage of the holiday home for neighbouring domestic servants.

We became good friends with Stefans and when he retired our friendship continued. Whenever we were in the area, we would visit him in his home. He lived on the side of a hill with no roads leading to his little traditional Zulu hut, so we drove as far as we could across the grassy fields, amongst the grazing cattle, and walked the rest of the way.

We supported Stefans and supplemented his meagre pension until he passed away. His dependants were very impoverished, and after his death we continued to support the family. They attended the local church and we became involved with supplying the Sunday school of that church with gifts and sweets at Christmas and little treats throughout the year. The family could not speak English but thankfully, Gavin speaks Zulu and so there was no need for an interpreter.

While chatting with the family one day, Stefans' daughter, a woman now approaching middle age, mentioned in the conversation that she had never owned a bed. She had slept on the floor all her life and as she approached her senior years this was becoming very uncomfortable for her.

We were shocked. It was not something we had thought about. We presumed all family members had beds. Once we were aware of the situation, we had no peace until we did something about it. We bought her a beautiful three quarter size base and mattress. The look of shock was something to behold when we told her a bed was being delivered.

We drove to Kwa Zulu Natal twice per year on outreach. We took hundreds of Zulu tracts with us as well as Easter eggs or sweeties and buckets of groceries for the old folks. As we drove along the roads, the length of our southeast coast from the border with Mozambique right down to the border with the Transkei, we gave children tracts and sweets and old folks' tracts, a bucket of groceries and some money.

We met some very interesting characters while doing this.

One old man who could only be described as a "wondering minstrel", with no fixed abode, would wonder from place to place strumming a self-made guitar, comprising of an old oil can, scraps of wood and wire.

The wandering minstrel with his home made guitar.

It was not always safe to be in these areas. There was a lot of political unrest and emotions could run high. On one occasion, as we were about to enter an area, we met a doctor racing away in his car. He warned us not to go into the village at that time, as he had just been shot at. He showed us the place where the bullet was still lodged in the upright between the two windows of the vehicle!

Another young missionary was delivering food hampers to

an AIDS orphanage and lost his way. When he stopped to ask for directions, he was summarily shot dead and thrown out of his car, which was then stolen by the killers.

Kwa Zulu Natal had the highest incident of HIV aids in the world. We often came across heart breaking scenarios of a child no older than perhaps twelve or thirteen, acting as the head of a family, trying to provide for as many as six or seven siblings. More often though, we would find a granny, her own children long since dead, caring for numerous grandchildren on her meagre state pension. Although we did not feel led to get involved in an AIDS ministry, we always did our best to try and bring a measure of relief when we found needs.

Most of the men living in these remote villages became migrant workers as local employment was scarce or non-existent. They would leave their wives and children to look after the village hut, toil the fields, care for the cattle, and generally fend for themselves. While the men were away, raiders from neighbouring Transkei would swoop down and steal the cattle, rob the homes and sometimes harm the inhabitants of the village. Because they were cross-border raids, the culprits would disappear across the boundary line between the two countries, and it was difficult for the authorities to put a stop to it. Many people suffered great losses as a result.

We befriended a minister who was put in charge, by his denomination, of planting churches in the Transkei. Although we did not work in the Transkei, we supported Richard Sekoe in all his efforts and still support him today.

We felt a desire to get involved with a needy church in the region of northern Natal but were not sure where, and didn't know of such a church. In one of our conversations with Richard, we mentioned this to him. He told us of a man who was trying to plant a church in a rural village near the town of Pongola. He gave us the Pastor's details and we were able to make contact.

Thembinkosi Kubheka was a trained Pastor who had secular employment while trying to build up a congregation in the rural village of Kwa Lubisie. He lived a three hour car journey away from the village and every week end he, his wife and infant daughter would make the long journey. We met up with Thembinkosi and told him that we wanted to help him in any way that we could. He was amazed and said that he had been praying that the Lord would bring someone alongside to help him. It was a joy and a privilege to get involved in this new work. Thembinkosi took us to an open piece of ground which had been earmarked for a church building.

With great joy and enthusiasm, he walked us around the perimeters of the land, sharing with us his vision of a church building with classrooms for Sunday school etc. He told us that he already had a group of folks who met in the local school for Bible study, but it was difficult as he was the only one with a Bible. It just so happened, that we had a case of Zulu Bibles in the car. They had been there for quite a while and Gavin had been hanging on to them, for such an occasion as this! We were able to give him the Bibles and oh what a joy and delight! He was so excited and we promised to return regularly.

Pongola is approximately 500 kilometres from where we live, in an easterly direction, so it was not always feasible to go as often as we would have liked. We met with the congregation in the local school classroom on Sundays and Gavin would preach and teach there. The classroom was far from ideal. The desks were the old fashioned kind, where the wooden table and chair were fastened together. The large African men would have to try and squeeze into these tiny desks designed for children and it was very uncomfortable. The classroom itself was a sad woe begotten excuse for a place of learning. The cement floor was pitted and cracked, as were the walls, which were naked of any posters or pictures. It got incredibly hot and stuffy in the little classroom with so many people crammed in it, but it was still a joy to be there.

Mrs Nomsa Kubeka at the new keyboard.

Our African people love to sing and are naturally gifted in this area. They could sing without accompaniment beautifully, but they do so love the keyboard! We were able to provide a keyboard for the Kwa Lubisie congregation as well as all the necessary cables and speakers. This, Nomsa, Thembinkosi's wife, would play on a Sunday, with the volume turned as high as possible. The singing was robust and loud. All and sundry could hear the melodies coming from the little school classroom and that in itself was an advert for the church!

Sunday school material was exceedingly difficult to procure. There were masses of curriculum available in English, but very little—and at times absolutely nothing—available in Ethnic languages. I felt strongly that it was wrong to give a six or seven year old child, Sunday school work sheets in anything other than their home language. Sunday school was meant to be fun and not to feel like school! After much searching we were only ever able to find material in the Zulu and Xhosa languages. We supplied the Kwa Lubisie Church with teacher's manuals as well as children's work books for the entire Sunday school for the whole year. We also provided Zulu Bibles for all in the church who needed them and started a building fund as well.

Sunday school material continues, to this day, to be a huge problem unless given in the English language. We have tried to get material translated in to ethnic languages but the cost makes this prohibitive for a small mission organization like ourselves.

The problems don't stop there either. Once material had been procured, the children need stationery to be able to complete the questionnaire, colour in the picture or complete a craft. If crafts are involved, then scissors, glue sticks and paper all need to be provided. As most Sunday schools meet outside, they need tables for the children to work at, thereby making a supply of lapboards necessary. The task seems almost insurmountable but Sunday school needs to be a place where children, "hear, see and do." This is how little minds work and little hearts are opened to the Gospel. These children are the future of the church in our land and we need desperately to continue seeking an answer to this complex problem.

Another difficulty is the issue of cultural relevance. At one point I ordered Sunday school material from America, intending it to be used in some of our rural Sunday Schools. When it arrived I avidly read through it and sadly realized that there was no possibility of ever using the material. The lessons mentioned, iPods, television, ballet lessons and violin playing—all of which had absolutely no meaning to a rural African child. We formulated our own material incorporating daily situations and things that a child in this setting can relate to and understand.

As mentioned earlier, Africans in general, especially in rural areas viewed animals as having various jobs to do and not as pets to be loved and spoiled. When Thembinkosi enquired after our family, I had to explain that besides Deanne we had a child who was slightly different. He was perplexed at first until we explained that our "special child" had four legs, long ears and a curly tail. We would take our beloved dog, little "Whisper", into the classroom with us for the church service, as it was too hot to leave her in the car. She would either sit on my lap or sit on a pillow on a chair beside me. She was always exceptionally well behaved and was accepted by the folks of the church as one of us.

At the conclusion of the services, we would stand just outside of the classroom door and shake everyone's hand as they were leaving. I would have Whisper under one arm and, without exception, everyone would shake her little paw as well. This was a huge concession from folks who do not view dogs in the same way that we do!

In the extremely remote areas, far from any cities or towns, we would come across children who were very afraid of us. We came to the conclusion that we were either the first white people they had seen or were the first white people to try and interact with them. Either way it was sometimes a daunting task to get the children to trust us enough to be able to engage with them.

We won the trust of these children.

It often helped to hold out a sweet to show we meant no harm. In a group of children, it only took the bravest child to come forward first and grab the sweet, for the others to realise we were not going to hurt them. Once this happened we would be rushed by the group all trying to grab the sweets out of our hands all at once. When they calmed down, we were able to give out gospel tracts as well. It was not often that people would come bearing gifts, so they were very receptive to the tracts and would eagerly read the paper, all in their own language.

In these remote areas, public transport was non-existent. Open back pickup trucks would be used to transport children to and from school. This, of course, was exceedingly dangerous as it offered the children no protection of any kind. We would see children crammed so tightly on these pickups that there was standing room only.

When the vehicle would stop to let a child off, we would draw up alongside it and distribute sweets and tracts. The response was always the same—little hands reaching out in eagerness to receive anything that was on offer.

Children eagerly reaching out for a tract and a gift.

Chapter 6

The Gospel River Ministry

Gavin has always been an outdoor fellow. I, on the other hand, prefer indoor activities and am very much a city born and bred type of character. Gavin loves fishing and boating and I love ballet and crafts!

While ministering to folks in the rural areas, we realized that some places were exceedingly difficult to reach by road. It would be easier to reach far flung villages by boat. Gavin, in his younger years before going into the ministry had a boat, but sold it to fund the work. He always hoped that one day he would be in a position to replace the vessel. We saved our meagre pennies for about twenty years before he was finally able to purchase a small boat. We started to use the vessel for ministry purposes by trying to navigate up small streams and rivers looking for remote villages.

There were many innate dangers relating to this part of the work. We had crocodiles and hippo's living in some of the rivers and sharks living in others. The boat we were using was a streamlined speedboat that offered no protection from the elements or from dangers such as these animals. I was very wary of hippo's in particular, as I had two great uncles who were in a boat which was capsized by a hippo and both men were killed.

When sharing about our work in Scotland one year, the people were horrified to hear that we were not using a more robust type of boat for this work. They wanted to support our efforts and encouraged Gavin to change the boat for one with a small cabin. This would provide a measure of protection for us from both the weather and wild animals. Gavin found a boat that met these requirements and the boats were duly exchanged. We named the vessel "The Sharon Rose".

Launching facilities were virtually unheard of, so Gavin would have to wade into the water to take the boat off its trail-

Gavin launching "The Sharon Rose".

er. I would sit in the boat or watch from the banks trying to see under the water. I would look for anything unusual, something that looked like a log could quite easily be a crocodile; air bubbles floating to the surface was a sure sign of a hippo under the water. If I saw any of these phenomena, I would shout to Gavin and he would leave the water as quickly as possible.

After launching the boat, Gavin would piggyback me to the vessel so that I did not get wet. There were occasions when he either lost his grip or his balance and both of us would land in the water and be thoroughly soaked.

I hated the boat with a passion! This was not my idea of fun. I hated the smell of the burning fuel, the movement of the boat made me seasick, and being out in the open was utter misery for me. But we were reaching more people with the Gospel, and I would say as King David said in the Bible, "Would I give to God that which cost me nothing?"

We were in Kwa Zulu Natal one year and were getting ready to launch the boat when a local man came up to us and asked if we were seriously going to put the boat in the water. We answered, "Yes, we were about to launch." He told us that two days prior to our arrival, a young village woman had been washing clothes at the very spot in the river where we were standing. She had her young son with her and as she bent down to rinse the clothing in the river, a crocodile had hurled itself out of the river and taken her. No evidence of the woman had since been found. We stood on the banks of that river for a long time but eventually did not launch the boat that day.

We used the boat in the Cape Province as well. A lot of rivers flow into the ocean from this region and one could travel quite far into the interior from there. At one particular spot we heard rumours of a monster living in the river. We knew the locals were superstitious and took no notice of what they said and used the boat on that river. A week later we returned home, turned on the television, and were shocked to see a program headed, "The Breede River Monster."

There had indeed been a monster in the river! Fishermen had been complaining of feeling a pull on their line only for the line to go slack a second later. When reeled in, the fishermen found just the head of a fish with the whole body missing and huge teeth marks gouged into the remaining flesh. Eventually, a team of marine biologists were called to investigate. After time passed, they caught the biggest bull shark ever recorded. It was a world record. The biologists took measurements and photographs, then released the shark back into the water at the very spot where we had launched our boat a mere week earlier.

Safety rules were beginning to be enforced as there had been a spate of boating accidents. All people wishing to place a boat on the water were required to be in possession of a skippers licence and all boats had to have a seaworthy certificate. The skipper's licence was a daunting task for Gavin as it entailed a two and a half hour examination, and he did not feel confident at all. But he needn't have worried. I was so proud of my husband, who passed the exam with ninety-six per cent.

The seaworthy certificate was a whole other story. It cost a small fortune to acquire all that was compulsory.

One of the prerequisites for this seaworthy certificate was called a floatation certificate. This stated that the boat had been filled with foam in the hull to make it virtually unsinkable. Without this document no seaworthy certificate would be issued. Each year the boat had to go through a series of tests and we had to produce all the relevant documentation. One year the official doing the test insisted that he needed the floatation certificate to process the annual license.

We very reluctantly handed it over to him with the promise that he would return it within seven days. Seven days came and went, seven weeks, then seven months. We kept phoning the official, nagging and pleading for the certificate, knowing that if it was not returned we would have serious problems the following year.

We were fobbed off at every turn with all sorts of excuses, until eventually the official wouldn't take our calls and refused to phone us back. We suspect he mislaid the document and it was incredibly difficult to replace. When the existing licence lapsed we could not get the boat seaworthy again. For eighteen months the boat stood without us being able to use it. We prayed much about the situation and were very frustrated at not being able to do that part of the work. Finally, our prayers were answered when we took advice from a boat dealership that dealt with officialdom, and they managed to procure another flotation certificate for us.

Whisper would accompany us on all the boat journeys and even had her own little life jacket that matched ours! Her life jacket had two handles on the back. This made it easier, if she fell into the water, to be plucked out by the handles on her back. Thankfully, we never had to do this and the life jacket was just a necessary "in case" piece of equipment.

Whisper with us on outreach.

Chapter 7

Clandestine Ministry in China

In the early 1990's Gavin was doing clandestine evangelism into China. I did not feel called to accompany him as he was smuggling Bibles from Hong Kong into China. I do not hide my feelings very well and the look of terror on my face would have been a dead giveaway to any authority! I could serve best by staying in South Africa and keeping the mission wheels turning.

On his first trip into China, he was taken to a safe house in Hong Kong. Along with a group of other people from different countries, he was given Bibles to be carried across the border into China. They were advised of the best possible way to smuggle the Bibles and some people opted for concealing them on their person, under their clothing, or ladies would sew them into their skirts.

However, my husband, a very large man, did not have the option of doing this. He was far too big. He prayed for wisdom and finally placed a camera around his neck and carried the camera bag filled with Bibles over his shoulder.

To create a diversion when entering the country, he decided to pretend to drop all of his papers at customs and hopefully distract the officials from the bag on his shoulder. When he finally approached the customs official, he genuinely dropped all his papers.

Bending down to retrieve the documents, he noticed that the clips on the sides of the bag, which held the straps in place, had pulled open with the added weight of the Bibles. The bag was in imminent danger of coming unclasped and the contents would have spilled out onto the customs floor in front of the officials.

He was so shocked that, without thinking, he picked up his papers, put his arm under the bag and just walked through customs without ever placing the bag on the x-ray machine! He said that he could feel the scornful eyes of the officials boring into him, but they did not accost him. Finally, after much earnest prayer he made it safely through the border with all the Bibles intact. There were many more trips, each with a story to tell, but that was the most harrowing one for Gavin.

These were the days before international travel had become cheaper and easier. Few Chinese had seen westerners and Gavin stood out from the rest due to his large frame. People would stare at him as he passed by. At one point, the group passed a ladies hairdressing salon. When the hairdressers saw Gavin they came running out to him giggling, leaving their clients with curlers falling out of their hair and onto the floor. They surrounded him, and splaying their hands, tried to put their fingers around the tops of his knees. They felt the hair on his arms and played with his beard. He said he felt like a dinosaur that had just been discovered! The group with him found the whole episode extremely funny and teased him relentlessly about the incident.

The Chinese were curious about Gavin because of his size and appearance, and because he always wore a large cross around his neck. It gave him a wonderful opportunity to talk about Jesus, as folks would walk up to him, point to the cross, and ask its meaning.

Distribution of Gospel tracts was prohibited in China and Gavin took an awful risk doing this. While he was there, a group of Chinese missionaries had been jailed for doing the very same thing. He would tell of incidents where with heart pounding, he would give tracts to the locals at the train stations and on the streets.

One group of young people he befriended sold food from kiosks on one of the platforms of the train station. Gavin would buy water from them before boarding a train and again upon his return. They would, on occasion, even share their packed lunches with him. On one journey a police official noticed that Gavin was giving Gospel tracts to the locals and accosted him. The young people at the Kiosks could see the trouble looming ahead and quickly intervened. They started to distract the police official by playing with his tie and making a general nuisance of themselves. While the official was shouting at them, another young person grabbed Gavin and whisked him away down a side alley and he made his escape. Gavin was a marked man and from then on had to be extremely careful in all his dealings while in China.

Gavin started to hear rumours of what today is known as "the dying rooms". China had a one-child policy. If a woman fell pregnant with a second child, enormous pressure was brought to bear on her to have an abortion. The family would be heavily fined if they did not adhere to this policy. Sons carried on the family name and were highly valued. If a son was born, there would be great celebrations with fireworks; if a girl was born, she was often not wanted. Many little girls were just dumped at state orphanages.

The survival rate of those with special needs was low due to neglect and ignorance of the officials caring for them. The so called "dying rooms" were places where baby girls were left to die. Authorities strongly denied this was taking place, but the rumours persisted. Gavin, being tender hearted, had no peace after hearing this allegation and he needed to find out for himself if it was true.

After much searching and asking around, Gavin heard of an American Christian man who had been allowed to visit one of the orphanages and was still volunteering in that institution. Gavin managed to track this person down and persuade the man to take him along on his next trip.

That visit had a profound effect on Gavin and changed his life. After all the horrors we had both witnessed in South Africa, this seemed even worse to him. He saw children tied into so-called potty chairs where they would be left to sit for hours.

Children were chained with padlocks to their cots, stopping

them from getting out and running about. What the children all had in common, he said, was that they would sit and rock to and fro. He never saw any tiny babies, but there was a section of the orphanage where they were not permitted to enter.

A young Irish woman, who had accompanied Gavin, unbeknown to him had managed to slip away from the group and took two photos of tiny baby girls in the prohibited section. She didn't confess to Gavin at the time that she had done so. Years

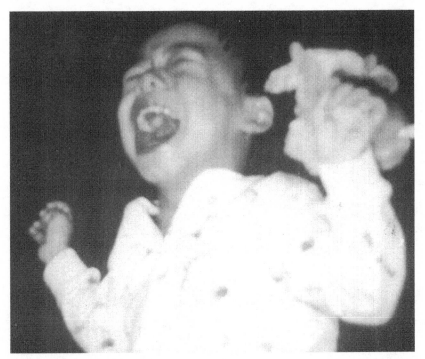

One of the photo's provided by the Irish girl.

later we met up with this same girl in Ireland and she produced the photographic evidence of what she had seen. She gave Gavin copies of the photos she had taken.

The children were absolutely starved of love and would hang on Gavin's legs just for a bit of attention and affection.

He said the carers who worked with the children had been placed there by the state and it was obvious that they had no love for the little ones and treated them as objects.

In 1995 a team of British journalists from the BBC infiltrated some of the orphanages with hidden cameras in their bags and managed to film the reality of all the rumours and more. Their documentary aired on television, and it horrified the western world. There was a huge backlash because of this incident and one of the repercussions was a clamp down on all foreign visitors to the orphanages. Gavin's contact was refused permission to return to the orphanage that he had been working in for a number of years, and all doors seemed to have closed.

The following year, Gavin was determined to go back and gain entry into one of the orphanages. After a huge struggle, he finally found a taxi driver willing to take him to one of these institutions well outside of the city limits.

They drove for many miles until eventually the vehicle pulled up alongside a huge nondescript looking building. The taxi drove off, leaving Gavin outside in the road. He walked up to the front door and knocked. The woman answering the knock spoke a bit of English, so Gavin could communicate with her. She was very curious about him and wanted to know where he was from and what he was doing there. That gave him a foot hold to start chatting to her.

She eventually invited him in to her office and they had a long conversation. She finally agreed to show Gavin around and allowed him to spend some time with a large group of mentally disabled children. He had brought with him a suitcase filled with new children's clothes, tooth brushes and various other items which she was glad to receive. Although the door was closed for others, Gavin was grateful to have been allowed back and to spend time with the children.

Giving gifts to the orphans.

Although the backlash to the BBC's documentary had been severe, eventually good came from the exposure of these places. Far reaching changes were later introduced to the orphanages. The uncaring officials had been replaced with well-trained caring young social welfare workers. The neglect and ill treatment of the children ended and outsiders were once again allowed back to visit.

Gavin went into China regularly over fifteen years. As mentioned earlier, he had come to the attention of the PSB (the secret police in China at that time) and throughout those years had to stay one jump ahead of the authorities. He would have to stay in far flung places, out of the city limits, and keep a low profile.

Over the ensuing years, conditions did improve for some believers. Bibles, which previously were only allowed to be owned by members of "The Three Self", state-sanctioned church, were now available to all. In certain regions Bible smuggling became a thing of the past. Gavin felt that the improvements were of such a nature that the funding used for the China outreach could be better used elsewhere in the ministry, so the work in China came to an end.

Chapter 8

Israel: Not All It Seems

Three young Irish lads that Gavin met in China encouraged him to go across to Ireland to share about the work in South Africa. Gavin does nothing without a lot of prayer and upon his arrival back home; we started praying about going abroad to Ireland. Finances for the ministry were always tight and we were a faith based ministry, living from hand to mouth. We did not receive a salary and had nothing to call our own. Everything that was bought was owned by the ministry and international funding would help us tremendously.

We prayed for three years before we felt the Lord prompting us go. Paying for the air tickets took what little finances were available with hardly anything left over for foreign exchange and other needs. We planned to go for six weeks, visiting firstly the contacts Gavin had made in China with the Irish lads, then on to England where we were invited by a young couple in our home church who had moved to London. We were also asked to visit Scotland by a Scottish lady who had worked in South Africa with Youth for Christ. So it was by invitation that we finally went to the United Kingdom for the first time.

Gavin's brother was a missionary working in Israel and we managed to acquire a free stopover in Israel on route. It had been my life's ambition, up until that point, to go to Israel in order to walk the streets where Jesus had walked all those years ago.

Upon our arrival at Ben Gurion airport in the evening, we collected our hired car and started to head towards the town of Joppa, where we had booked accommodation for the night. As Gavin is diabetic, we needed to find a shop to buy him something to eat. We found our way through the busy streets to a supermarket of sorts and parked right outside the front door. Knowing we wouldn't be long, we left all our belongings in the vehicle and entered the shop. We bought a few snacks of what seemed to us something akin to what we would normally consume and made our way to the exit.

Coming out onto the busy street, we couldn't find the hired car! We searched and searched but came to the conclusion it had been stolen. My heart sank into the pit of my stomach as I realised that all our luggage, but more importantly our passports, air tickets and most of our foreign exchange was all locked up in that vehicle.

In blind panic and sheer terror we started to ask passers-by what to do. Most couldn't speak much English but eventually one very kind gentleman helped us to call a taxi. He instructed the taxi driver to take us to the nearest police station.

After an incredibly long and anxious wait, we were finally ushered forward to the front desk. Battling to make ourselves understood, the policeman eventually entered our details into the computer.

We discovered that no, the car had not been stolen but had been impounded by the authorities! When parking our vehicle we had forgotten that the Jewish language is written from right to left, not from left to right as we do. This meant that the no parking sign actually meant the opposite of what we had read it to mean; thereby we had inadvertently parked in the times that were expressly forbidden.

We were forced to pay a ridiculously high fine to have the car released from impound and then pay another taxi driver to take us to the outskirts of the city to the large enclosure where impounded vehicles were kept. By this time it was extremely late; we were exhausted and longed to climb into bed for some rest. These were the days before Sat Nav and since we were on the wrong side of Tel Aviv we had to find our way to Joppa. It goes without saying that we got hopelessly lost and finally arrived at our destination at 4 am utterly spent, stressed and miserable.

In the light of day the next morning we noticed huge scratch marks where the car had been lifted by massive claws when impounded the previous evening. We had the added burden of the cost of re-spraying the vehicle over the damaged areas.

We made our way to Jerusalem where we stayed in the Christian quarter of the old walled city. It was ideally situ-

ated for us, being close to the many historical places that I
was yearning to see. There were so many sights and sounds
that were alien to us—the wail of the Muslim call to prayer,
the many shopkeepers hawking their wares and the throngs
of tourists milling about in the Arab markets. I was chomping
at the bit to be let lose to explore Herod's Palace, the Western
Wall, the Temple Mount, the Garden tomb, the Via Dolorosa,
the Mount of Olives, Mount Zion and the many Churches that
scattered the landscape.

We took the next week to explore to our hearts content
and were bitterly disappointed with all we discovered. Many
folks are shocked when we share this with them. After all,
most tourists who go to Israel have a wonderful and blessed
experience. It must be remembered that we were not part of
an organised tour group and basically lived with the locals as
one of them.

We did not see the touristy Israel, but saw a more realistic
and down-to-earth Israel that has extremely complex problems. But we were searching for a spiritual experience and it
was not what we expected. Every church we visited was or-
nately decorated and had all the trappings of materialism attached to it. We never felt the holiness and reverence for which
we were searching. Both Gavin and I felt the Lord impressing
these words upon us: "Why seek ye the living among the dead?
I am not here I have risen."

Walking down the Via Dolorosa, I imagined it must have
been similar in the Lord's day, with the businesses open and
proprietors enticing folks in to come and look at their wares.
The stares from the Arab men at Western women was most

disconcerting and I did not feel comfortable. Every time we went out, I made sure I was well covered, keeping my eyes on the ground before me as I hung onto Gavin's arm, not letting go for a second.

On one particular day we visited the Church of the Holy Sepulchre. The church is built over the remains of Golgotha and also over the tomb where Christ was buried and rose again. Upon exiting the church we were accosted by a group of young people who were carrying platted crowns of thorns. These they shoved under our noses crying loudly, "Born again? Here buy— cheap, cheap!" This summed up for us that which was an affront to all we hold so precious and dear. It was a bitter experience.

We befriended a young German couple who expressed a desire to go up a nearby hill to pray over the city of Jerusalem. We offered to take them in our car and together we would pray for the city. We drove as close to the base of the hill as we could and then hiked the rest of the way up. It was a beautiful evening, and as the sun was setting the last rays of sunshine hit the stone buildings and turned them into a beautiful golden hue. It looked like a city of gold set upon a mountain. We had a time of prayer, and when it started getting dark we decided to head back down the hill.

We were about halfway down when we caught the first glimpse of our vehicle. It was surrounded by police vans with flashing blue lights. Yet again, blind panic set in and the hollow feeling in the pit of my stomach returned with a vengeance. I started running and stumbling down the hill as fast as I could on the uneven terrain screaming, "Don't take our car away, please don't take our car!" We finally arrived breathless and distraught, only to be told that we had accidently parked beside a secret military installation and the authorities thought that perhaps a car bomb had been planted there. After a thorough search of the vehicle, and relief beyond words, we drove back to the haven of our guest house.

On the Saturday of our stay, after a morning of siteseeing, we arrived back into the Christian quarter of the walled city to find there were no parking spaces to be had. We drove around the crowded streets, entering through the Jaffa gate and exiting the Dung gate, over again for ages, without being able to find somewhere to leave the car. It was extremely hot and eventually Gavin said that we should give up looking for a space and instead find a shop where we could buy a cold drink. This we did. In the process (we still don't know why or how), we managed to enter the Mea Shearim.

The Mea Shearim is an area in Jerusalem that is inhabited mainly by Haredi Jews who adhere to strict Jewish law. There are "Modesty" posters hung at building entrances and women are asked to wear modest attire—no plunging necklines, no sleeveless blouses and no midriff tops. During Shabbat, from sunset Friday until Saturday night, barriers are placed across the entrances to keep people from driving into the area.

We had no idea that we had entered the Mea Shearim, but we soon found out. A group of six or seven young boys, complete with long peyotes (the sideburns that are usually curled and hang loose down the sides of their little faces), and black hats, formed a barrier against us. They were holding hands and stretched out in a line across the road barring us from going any further. The young boys started hissing and spitting at us. Some bent down, picked up stones, and started flinging them at the car. We were in deep trouble and didn't know what to do.

Just then a Rabbi came around a corner and assessing the situation quickly pointed for us to follow him. He directed us to an exit and cleared the barrier enabling us to leave. We never meant to cause offense and it was innocently done, so the vehemence of the retribution took us by surprise.

We visited with Gavin's brother in the town of Katzrin on the Golan Heights. As we entered his home, the first thing to greet us was a staircase going down into the bomb shelter! Because we were there over Yom Kippur, we did not go out or visit any sites but stayed indoors and enjoyed time with the family.

Upon our return to Jerusalem we were accommodated by a Messianic Jewish friend named Tony. His house bordered the boundary with the Mea Shearim, and on our last evening in Israel, he took us to a nearby café for a meal. We sat at an outside table and enjoyed our last sights, sounds and smells of this unique place.

After a delicious meal we started to hear what sounded like a huge angry mob. Tony denied this saying it was just revellers and we were to ignore it. After the meal, we headed back to Tony's house for a cup of coffee before leaving for the airport. As we started walking towards the boundary with the Mea Shearim we got caught up in a thirty thousand strong protest march by the Orthodox Jewish community. They were protesting against Yitzhak Rabin signing the peace accord with the Arab nation and the giving away what they called, "God given land."

This happened within months of my own shooting and I was still experiencing post-traumatic stress syndrome. To be caught up in a throng of this magnitude was frightening. Added to the terror that I was experiencing was the sense of imminent danger as many of the protestors were carrying torches with naked flames. If one person had fallen or dropped their flame it could have had a knock on effect with dire consequences. Hyper ventilating, and with heart pounding, I buried my face against Gavin's shoulder blades, tucked my hands in his belt and my extremely large husband pushed and elbowed his way through the masses. We were unable to reach Tony's house the way we would normally go and were forced to cut through the Mea Shearim. As I was not expecting to enter this area, I had worn a sleeveless blouse because of the extreme heat. The looks of pure disgust and thinly veiled hatred that were thrown my way are forever etched in my memory.

With a huge sigh of relief, we sat down in Tony's home and had a cup of coffee. When it was time to leave for the airport, Tony offered to walk with us to our car which was parked a fair distance away. He instructed us to walk on ahead while he locked up his home. Arm in arm, Gavin and I strolled down the walkway, excited thoughts of home filling our minds. All of a sudden an Israeli soldier in full combat gear ran up to us and shouted at us in a language we could not understand. Both Gavin and I smiled shrugged our shoulders and gestured that we didn't understand. The soldier, in extreme agitation, shoved Gavin in the chest with a mighty force screaming,

"Bomb, bomb!" A car bomb had been discovered just a few meters from where we were going to step off of the pavement. A few seconds later a second soldier rushed behind the first, unravelling chevron tape to cordon off the road. We were forced to walk many kilometres in a detour to reach our vehicle.

I have never been so pleased to flop down on an aeroplane seat knowing I was leaving a country. I have no intention of ever visiting Israel again unless my Master expressly commands it!

Chapter 9

Lay Your All on the Altar of Sacrifice

Our first trip to the United Kingdom was a huge leap in faith as we only had enough funding for the first two weeks of our six week stay and had huge gaps in our itinerary. I was reminded of the book title –"If you want to walk on water, you have to get out of the boat!" It took a huge dependency upon the Lord, not knowing how we were going to survive after the initial two week period.

Once again, through miraculous circumstances, doors opened for us into churches as well as homes. We started to receive funding for the work and built up a support base. From the onset though, we felt that we did not want to just take aid from the UK and Ireland but wanted to give something back in return.

The Lord made this possible when we began to receive invitations for Gavin to preach in many churches and for us to minister in schools, retirement homes and hospitals. It has always been the policy of Rose of Sharon, never to go knocking on doors to find support for the Lord's work. Instead, we trusted the Lord to touch the hearts of those of his people through whom he wanted to provide for this, His work.

Also, instead of relying on our own best efforts to open doors, we prayerfully undertook never to approach any church, Christian group or Christian organization. We would only go in response to an invitation from God's people. In this way we were always assured that it was God opening the door for us from his side through his people.

The more doors that opened for us, the longer we had to stay in the UK and Ireland. This meant leaving family, friends—and of course our wonderful little dog, Whisper. Being a homebody, I started finding these trips ever more difficult. Eventually, we were invited to so many churches that we were spending five and a half months of every year travelling around the UK and Ireland, Gavin preaching and us doing mission type meetings with PowerPoint presentations about the work in South Africa. Today, eighty per cent of the funding for The Rose of Sharon comes from Scotland, Ireland and England. We see God's plan so clearly unfolding in our lives as this is not something we would ever have dreamed of doing ourselves.

Huge sacrifices have been made over the years in order to live this kind of lifestyle. When we started travelling abroad roughly twenty years ago both Gavin and I were a lot younger and much healthier than we are today.

Gavin's diabetes has taken a toll on his health and although he struggles, not once has he ever had to withdraw from any part of the work and continues faithfully to do all the Lord has called him to do. I stand back amazed at my husband's fortitude in the face of his many difficult health issues. Over the years he has had a heart attack, two stents have been placed in his arteries and he struggles with high blood pressure and a host of other health issues.

Constantly moving from one area to another, living out of a suitcase for so many months at a stretch can be extremely difficult. Staying in countless, different homes, each with differing routines and a change of beds every few nights did have an effect. We jokingly say that we could write a book on the number of different beds that we have slept upon. Hard beds, soft beds, lumpy ones and squeaky ones – but we were grateful for each and every one.

A particularly memorable bed was in a caravan we were given to use on the east coast of Scotland. The mattress was supported by a series of wooden slats that were slotted into grooves on the inside of the base. The slats would sag with our combined weight until eventually, usually in the early hours of the morning, the slats would give way and we would find ourselves unceremoniously dumped on the floor.

Many a true word is said in jest and we would joke about not being able to have a proper "domestic." As we were always in the limelight, and staying in other people's homes, it would hardly be proper to have a fight! We landed up airing our disagreements in the car while travelling as it was the only place where we had a bit of privacy.

Homesickness would strike without warning. I missed Deanne so much. She stayed with family and was in very good care and lacked for nothing while we were away, but I was not there when she needed me and I battled with feelings of guilt and inadequacy.

I remember crying out, "Oh Lord, why did you make me a mother if I cannot be one?" The words from Scripture came to mind—"If you love Mother or Father more than me, you are not worthy of me". I felt hurt and angry as I watched my daughter struggle through her teenage years without a mother's council and companionship for six months of every year. I missed so much of her growing into adulthood. I was not there when she had her wisdom teeth taken out, when she was ill or when she had school exams. I was not able to do the usual things a mother does for her daughter. This has had far reaching consequences, and although we are exceptionally close as mother and daughter, this one thing stands between us.

There were times that I would have given everything I had to be able to stay at home or if away, go home. One year while we were in Scotland, Deanne became ill and was hospitalized. As a mother, everything in me screamed to go home and be at my daughter's bedside. It was not an option financially as there was no possibility of a return ticket back to the UK.

I would Skype with her, and through the haze of medication one morning, she told me that she would listen to the footsteps coming down the hospital corridor and look at the door of the ward, hoping to see me walk through it. Those words broke my heart and still haunt me to this day.

My daughter married in 2005. Deanne and her husband

had been dating for eleven years and he was her first and only boyfriend. It was a beautiful ceremony, but here too, I was left out of some of the things that the mother of the bride would normally do. I simply was not there to do them. After a few years Deanne and Donovan decided to start a family. This was the beginning of years of pain and heartache, many hospital stays and surgical procedures.

A few days before we were due to leave for the UK in 2009, we received the news that she had fallen pregnant. We knew this was not going to be an easy pregnancy and I was frantic to be with her. Our flights were booked and the itinerary set—there was no backing out at that late stage. I prayed and prayed for this unborn child. I was duly sent photos of the scans and kept in contact with Deanne almost daily. I had a strange calmness that all would be well and had absolute faith that the child would be healthy.

The pregnancy developed, and towards the end of our trip I was so excited to be going home and to see my daughter in her "preggie" dresses and to place my hand on her stomach and feel my granddaughter kick. I felt that I had missed out on so much of the pregnancy but would finally be able to make up for it once we arrived home.

A few days before we were due to fly back to South Africa, at six o' clock one morning, I received a message on my mobile phone. It read "baby didn't make it, I'm so sorry".

"What?"my mind screamed. I just couldn't comprehend what I was reading. I had somehow convinced myself that because we were on "our King's business" that He would look after and protect my daughter and granddaughter. I felt let down, that a line in the sand that I had drawn had been crossed. No promises had been made to me stating this, but it was something about which I had convinced myself. This episode led to a dark period in my spiritual walk with the Lord. It took many months of soul searching before I found peace and restitution with my saviour.

Three years later, Deanne did give birth to a little girl who is the apple of her granny's eye and I thank the Lord for answered prayer in His good and perfect time.

My dear daughter Deanne and Granddaughter Mikayla.

My aging mother was becoming increasingly frail. Because we were out of the country for nearly half of every year, we knew that there was a risk of her passing away while we were not in South Africa.

Once again I prayed that the Lord would not take her while

we were in the UK. In 2014, we had been out of South Africa for a mere two weeks when we received the devastating news that she had very suddenly passed away. I was thrown into a quandary. At that stage of our trip we were in the furthest point of the Outer Hebrides, and it would have taken four flights back to Cape Town for me to attend the funeral, and then four flights to return to the Hebrides. Financially, this was out of the question. Also, there were issues about our visa restrictions. I didn't know if I would be allowed back into the country again so soon after leaving it. One of our supporting churches kindly offered to pay the costs for me to travel home but because of the visa concerns, it was finally decided that I would not go back for the funeral. Not attending my own mother's funeral was one of the hardest things I have ever faced.

Before our darling little Whisper came into our lives, we had another beloved Maltese named Muffin. Deanne kindly opened her home to Muffin while we travelled abroad. Muffin lived to the ripe old age of sixteen years. We were in Scotland on the Isle of Lewis when Deanne sent us news of her sad passing. Once again I was denied the opportunity of saying my last farewells.

I vowed never to have another dog again since I had loved Muffin so much and believed that I could never love another as much. Upon our return to South Africa that year, the loss of Muffin was keenly felt. There was no furiously wagging tail to greet us when arriving home, no warm weight upon my lap when sitting down and no pint sized, furry little body to snuggle down with at night. Gavin would urge time and time again,

"Let's get another dog, please let's get another dog!"

Eventually we started praying about the matter. It was extremely important for us to acquire the "right" dog, in terms of temperament and behaviour. Our dog needed to be highly adaptable, going with us to so many different places, being touched by many children and used as an illustration in many different settings. Basically, we needed a dog we could trust to always be on her best behaviour and to be loving and gentle.

After many weeks of praying and looking, we still had not found a dog that we felt was suitable. One Saturday morning Gavin told me that he had a strong leading to go to the local Pound. I was absolutely horrified! I didn't want someone else's' "cast off", or a dog with emotional baggage. It was with great reluctance that I accompanied my husband that morning.

The local Pound is huge, with rows and rows of cages with sometimes two and three dogs in each cage. We proceeded to row one and in cage one, a little Maltese came toddling out. I took one look at this dog and burst into tears. "I can't do this!" I cried, and I ran back to the car.

Gavin stayed with this little dog and played with her for a while. He later came back to the car and asked me to have another look at her as she seemed very sweet. Reluctantly I went back. I had to admit she seemed to have the right temperament. We prayerfully decided that we would adopt her.

Upon arriving home with us, the little dog never made a sound. She didn't seem to be afraid, but would not bark and made herself as unobtrusive as possible. Thus, we named her "Whisper".

Looking back at those early stages with her, we realise now just how traumatized the wee mite must have been. She has subsequently found her voice, is rather loud at times, barking at all and sundry, but the name Whisper has stuck! She is a special dog and is exactly right for us and fits in perfectly with the ministry. Oh yes—I freely admit that I love her more than I ever loved Muffin!

These are just some incidents that give a glimpse into the personal difficulties we suffered while travelling but they do not negate the incredible blessings we have also experienced. In Mark 10: 28-31 of the Bible, Peter turned to Jesus and said, "Master, we have left everything to follow you."

Jesus answered, "I tell you the truth, no one who has left home or brothers or sister or Mother or Father or children for me and the Gospel will fail to receive a hundred times as much in this present age (homes, brothers, sisters, mothers, children and fields-and with them persecutions) and in the age to come eternal life."

We have found this to be our experience. The Lord has opened countless homes to us. We have friends who have become like mothers and fathers or brothers and sisters to us. The Lord has on occasion even provided a little dog here and there for me to cuddle when the longing for Whisper has become unbearable.

To God alone be the glory for what has done.

Chapter 10

Farewell to All Things Dear

There is always frantic rushing around and much preparing to be done before leaving our home for five and a half months. All food has to be removed as not even a crumb may remain in the house as one can imagine what the condition of food left for that length of time would be like. Electrical appliances all have to be switched off and unplugged and furniture covered with dust covers.

Huge amounts of groceries, sweets and other supplies have to be bought in and delivered to the local folks whom we stock pile to help them along while we are away. Emergency funds are given to them as well.

There is then, of course, the awful tearful goodbyes to family and friends. Saying goodbye to Deanne is the singular most difficult of all the goodbyes which leaves me broken hearted each year. I find this incredibly difficult because of the fragility of life in all its uncertainty, one never knows if and when we will be reunited.

When all is done we finally load up the vehicle with not only our suitcases but little Whisper's possessions as well. We joke that the Mutt has nearly as much baggage as we do! She has a staircase to allow her to climb onto the bed and now in her latter years, we have also provided her with a ramp which has made it easier than the stairs. She has a car seat which elevates her so that she can see out of the window while travelling if she is not sitting on "Mommy's lap". Whisper has a Papoose to be carried around in and also an assortment of beautiful jackets to adorn her sweet little plump frame.

Loaded too, are the many buckets of groceries to be given out along the route to the many needy old folks we encounter as well as tracts and sweet hampers for the children. The journey takes 2 days with a stopover night about half way through the journey. We encounter many heart breaking scenarios on these trips which have already been described in earlier chapters.

When we arrive in Fish Hoek we stay with my wonderful sister Heather and her little Yorkshire terrier named Klara. Whisper and Klara get on really well and a warm excited, waggly welcome is the order of the day. Whisper settles quickly into her usual little routine but very soon smells a rat when seeing suitcases being packed and then becomes very clingy refusing to let us out of her sight.

We also take aid of various kinds to the Tiny Tots Day Care Centre while we are there. We always enjoy our time with the kiddies who are so sweet and very different from the street wise hardened youngsters we work with in the shanty towns around the city of Johannesburg.

All too soon the day of departure arrives and with hearts breaking we say a sad farewell to Heather, Klara and our sweet little baby dog.

My kind sister Heather with doggies Klara (left) and our baby Whisper (right).

We usually have a couple of hiccups on our journey to the UK. This past year when I booked our seats online, the website warned that because we had a connecting flight, we needed to take our luggage receipts to the bag drop off point at

Oliver Tambo airport in Johannesburg. When we booked in at the flight desk in Cape Town I asked for the luggage receipts and explained why. I was told in no uncertain terms that it was not necessary and that the luggage had been booked straight through to Heathrow. Well, you guessed it—when we arrived in Johannesburg we were asked for our luggage receipts, which I didn't have. It was quite a problem as they tried to trace our bags and get them on the right flight. Oh, why can't anything work the way it's supposed to in South Africa? Thankfully, our luggage was found and rerouted to Heathrow.

After this debacle, we had to make our way from domestic arrivals to international departures, through security and to our departing gate, all in a space of 45 minutes. Because Gavin has difficulty walking long distances due to the nerve damage in his feet, a wheel chair had been organised for him. The gentleman pushing the wheel chair kept telling me that we needed to hurry as we didn't have a lot of time. I could barely keep up with him. I limp when forced to walk at speed, and I was carrying my on board luggage weighing 10kgs as well.

I was totally breathless when we arrived at international departures assisted travel counter. We now needed to change over from being helped by domestic wheel chair assistance to international wheel chair assistance. To our dismay, we were told that although they knew we were coming and all had been arranged, they did not have the staff to help us!

By this time we only had 5 minutes to boarding and the gate was a good 10 minute walk from where we were. In desperation I asked if I may push the wheel chair and was given the go ahead. So here I was, with my on board luggage weighing

10kgs on my back, pushing a wheel chair with a man weighing 150kgs, and on his lap was another 10kg bag and a 6 months supply of insulin.

I started to try and run pushing this lot, but as I was already tired from a very brisk walk from domestic arrivals, it just was not happening! Gavin insisted on getting out of the wheel chair and walking, but I insisted he stay where he was. By this time my legs felt like jelly and I knew that I could go no further.

Gavin grabbed the first African gentleman he could find wearing an airport uniform and offered him R50 to push the chair the rest of the way. What a relief to have some help! I barely made it to the plane, but we finally arrived while passengers were still boarding. By the time we found our seats I was huffing and puffing and the exertion of the past 40 minutes led to a mild asthma attack.

The flight was a terrible trial for Gavin, and I wondered how many more years we have left of him being able to travel. He has vowed that he cannot go home the same way we have come. As we can only afford economy class tickets, I am going to explore what avenues are open to us to try and give him a little more room on the plane. His hips are so bruised from the seats being so narrow that he can't fit into them. His legs and feet were incredibly swollen from not being able to stretch out properly. He spent quite a lot of time sitting on the temporary seat for the air hostesses in the galley as it has no sides or arm rests. But he couldn't sit there all the time as they also needed to work in the galley. I felt really sorry for him. My back is the only thing that plagues me. Since my operation I find sitting for long periods of time very uncomfortable. Thankfully, after eleven and a half hours we finally made it!

On arrival at Heathrow, I was, as usual, extremely nervous going through customs and passport control. Although I have nothing to hide, I have an irrational fear of authority and find this part of the journey the most stressful and difficult. I kept praying asking the Lord to confirm for me that this was most definitely His will for my life at this time, by allowing us to get through with the utmost of ease. Oh what little faith we have at times! I hang my head in shame and wish with all my heart that I could be bold and courageous just knowing that I am on the Kings business and that nothing will stop His will from being done.

With fear and trembling I approached passport control and was confronted with a jovial older gentleman who was friendly and helpful. After just one question about why we were in the UK, he stamped our passports and we were on our way to customs. We collected our bags and walked straight through with no one stopping us or even looking our way. Oh God, my God, why do I doubt your wonder working ways? You are so faithful in spite of my lack of faith, how good you are to us!

We then picked up our hired car and drove the 2-3 hour journey to Suffolk. We are hosted by a wonderful farming family who allow us the use of a caravan on their farm. They took us under their wing about 15 years ago and since then have been wonderful staunch allies of Rose of Sharon. They very kindly allow us to leave our car in one of the out buildings here on the farm, when we return to South Africa. Before arriving back in the UK each year, they also put the car through the

MOT and kindly pay the tax disc as well.

The farm is beautiful. There are many rasping calls from the plentiful pheasants that run about here. I always feel as though I would like to take a can of oil and pour it down their throats! The stream that runs next to the caravan is clean and clear and gurgles happily past our bedroom window. We have seen beautiful little bunnies as well and marvel yet again at the beauty that surrounds us.

Chapter 11

"I'll Take the High Road..."
Travelling to Scotland

O nce getting ourselves organised with collating all we have left inside our car here in the UK, and what we bring with us each year, we start the laborious task of sorting out mundane things like obtaining mobile phone SIM cards, picking up our new flyers from the printer and buying basic necessities. Then, of course, the same old complaints that I always moan about—the packing up and loading of the car. We have so much luggage—it's just awful!

It's not clothing mind you. We have two cases of clothing, but the rest is taken up with the video projector, 2 computers, a full size printer, cameras and pots and pans since we often stay in empty manses that are not equipped. We also have a stationary box and a box of food. We cannot buy new bottles of coffee, for instance, in every different place we stay, so certain groceries travel with us. On top of all this we have a huge amount of medication and 6 months' worth of insulin which has to be kept cool at all times—a logistical nightmare!

Once organised, and after the car is legally taxed and insured, we expressed our thanks to our hosts and headed north to Scotland. The drive is normally long and it usually takes us a whole day to reach Kirkintilloch where we stay. But it took much longer than it should have this year as Gavin really struggled to drive the car. Because of his diabetes he has nerve damage in his feet and has now lost the feeling in his left foot. He could not feel when pressing down on the clutch and occasionally his foot would inadvertently hit the brake at the same time and the car would jerk and shudder. It was a nightmare journey and Gavin has lost all confidence in driving a manual car.

We arrived in Kirkintilloch totally stressed and exhausted, knowing that something drastic had to be done. We didn't know what we were going to do because we did not have the finance to replace the vehicle with an automatic one.

On the Saturday we met with some very dear friends and went out for a meal with them. We had a wonderful time of reconnecting and fellowship over some delicious food. At the end of a lovely visit, we were given a substantial donation— enough to replace our vehicle! They did not know of our predicament but the Lord had prompted them. What a faithful God we serve!

With great rejoicing, we went "home" and started car hunting online. We found a few possibilities but we did have some other logistical problems to sort out first. We were booked on a ferry to North Uist on the Monday afternoon. This entailed a 6-hour drive to the ferry terminal in Uig on the Isle of Skye. We would not do anything about the car on the Sunday, so had no choice but to cancel the ferry on the Monday and reschedule for the Tuesday.

There is only one sailing on a Tuesday and that is at 2 pm, which would mean a very early start. We were happy to do that to give us Monday to try and find a car. It was a tall order to hope that we could find one, purchase it, get rid of the other car, get the paper work done, reinsure, pay the vehicle tax and then do the usual loading to be ready to leave by 6 am Tuesday morning!

Another wonderful friend, Frank, who is also a member of the board of trustees for Rose of Sharon, very kindly took us car hunting early on Monday morning. I had seen a car advertised on the Auto Trader web site that looked promising, so we decided to start there.

The garage selling the vehicle was in Lesmahago, about a 40 minute drive on the highway from Kirkintilloch. When we arrived the car was nowhere to be seen. After enquiring about it, we were told that the garage hadn't received the vehicle from the previous owner yet and so it wasn't even on the show room floor! We explained our predicament and agreed that if they could get the car for us that day, we would buy it unseen. This is not something we would normally do, but Gavin and I both had perfect peace about it and just knew it was the right thing to do. Frank took us back to Kirkintilloch where we had to unload the old car of everything still in it and then Gavin drove it back to Lesmahago. Upon arriving with the old car, we were given a small amount as a trade in and were told that the "new" car needed new front disc brake pads and these were being ordered and would be fitted later in the day. We just needed to wait. Needless to say, it was a long day, but while we waited, we changed the insurance, changed the owner registration of the car and of course paid for it.

It was 5 pm before all was sorted and we saw the car for the first time. We were absolutely delighted with it. It has been immaculately kept, and although 15 years old, you would never say so. It had only had one lady owner and there was a full service history. If this was in South Africa we would automatically say, "pull the other leg—one lady owner ha ha!" but here in the UK the number of people who have owned the vehicle is listed on the registration document of the vehicle, so there cannot be any deception.

Also, one could see the vehicle has been really looked after. So we climbed into our "new" Mercedes ML 320 automatic, with Gavin very confident because the vehicle is the same as he drives in South Africa. The whole cost of the vehicle with the tax and everything else was EXACTLY what we were given by our dear friends. We stand amazed at the wonder working power of our God.

With great excitement we climbed into the vehicle for the journey back to Kirkintilloch, only to get about two miles down the road when smoke started pouring out from the left hand front wheel. It was so thick that I actually thought the wheel was on fire! The smell of burning rubber was thick and pungent.

We pulled over; thankfully the vehicle had a red triangle in the boot which we placed in the road. As it was after 5 pm we were not sure what to do. I tried phoning the mechanic but there was no response. We are members of the AA but the membership is for a specific vehicle and we had not yet changed the membership over to the new one. I did so while sitting in the broken down car but was informed by the AA that it takes 24 hours for this to come into effect. We were at a loss and did not know what to do. Gavin felt a clear prompt from the Lord to phone other dear friends of ours, George and Gill, who live in Lesmahago.

What a delight and joy to get hold of Gill. Gavin asked her to go to the garage to see if she could find someone to help us. Gill promptly jumped into her car, drove to the garage and found someone still there. She organised for a mechanic to come and fetch the vehicle and then George and Gill came to find us, bringing their gorgeous little dog in tow.

While the mechanic looked at the problem, we all went out

Our rescue team, George and Gill.

for coffee. It turned out that the brake pad had not been fitted properly and once inserted correctly the car was ready to go. In the meantime we had such a lovely blessed time of fellowship with George and Gill. What started out as a disaster turned into a real blessing!

On top of that I also got a "doggie fix" as I was having serious withdrawal symptoms and needed a doggy cuddle badly! Oh Lord, thank you for such wonderful friends that became rescuing angels to us and for turning a real disaster into a blessing!

The car ran very smoothly after that and continues to be a delight to us. We finally arrived back in Kirkintilloch just after 8 pm. It was then time to pack up and load the car before eventually falling exhausted into bed well after midnight.

The day before—Sunday—we had two services, one at Mount Vernon and the second one in Carmyl, both on the East side of Glasgow. It is always slightly daunting doing the first meetings of the year as the presentation is new and untried and one has to get used to public speaking again in another country.

The only mishap was when I was given the microphone to pin on my blouse. The little sponge rubber top came off of the microphone head and rolled under the pew in front of us. So, in my high heels and skirt, crawling on all fours, I wiggled between the pews looking for the stupid little thing. Unfortunately, I couldn't find it anywhere and was starting to feel a tad panicky when one of the ladies sitting on the stage in the choir who must have been watching this carry on, came down off the stage picked up the dastardly thing and handed it to me.

The whole episode was rather embarrassing but also quite funny. Seriously though, both meetings went really well and we were welcomed back with open arms. It is humbling to be embraced by folks who really care about the suffering of our people and who care about the lost.

We were given the most amazingly beautiful flannel graph board and corresponding pictures of Biblical characters to use in our Sunday Schools back in South Africa.

It was a 4.30 am start Tuesday morning with the last minute things packed, house tidied and we were on the road by 6 am. What a joy the vehicle proved to be. She was powerful and a real work horse — big and strong enough to take our entire luggage with room to spare.

It was a beautiful drive and the air was crisp and clean. The scenery was spectacular. The mountains were clothed in Heather and capped in snow. Their reflection was mirrored in the cerulean blue waters of the Loughs below and one wanted to cry out at the beauty of God's creation. Although the Heather was not in bloom yet, there were lilies, ferns, poppies, daisies, foxgloves and a host of other flowers in proliferation and it was stunning.

Driving through Glencoe was particularly lovely. Looking at the remote vastness of the place sent my imagination into overdrive. I could just imagine wild rugged Scots with painted faces and kilts running amok through the barren expanse of the hills and valleys of Glencoe. But when one thinks of the true history it's actually very sad and the infamy of the Campbell's massacring the MacDonald's still lives on.

We finally arrived at the Ferry terminal in Uig on Skye to sail across to the Islands of North and South Uist, Benbecular and Berneray. This we would consider to be the first leg of our ministry trip to the UK each year.

Chapter 12

First Port of Call: The Uists

W e do find that the weather can be challenging and some years it has been absolutely awful! We have had gale force winds many days and the wind can be bitterly cold, coming down from the arctic. This makes the temperatures feel much colder, because of the wind chill factor. The temperatures mostly struggle to get into double figures and we do not often see them above 11 degrees Celsius.

When it rains, the droplets are driven by the wind and instead of falling down from the sky in a vertical manner; the rain comes at you horizontally. The wind drives freezing cold rain under your clothing, which feels like razor sharp needles that sting most uncomfortably.

In spite of the weather, the Islands are beautiful. The Uists are known for their diversity of natural flora. The flowers, when coming into bloom, explode into colour in the open fields. There are beautiful white swans on the loch and also many wild deer for which we are always looking out for. Most often we would see them at night, when coming home from a meeting. As we approach the longest day of the year, the days are incredibly long with the sun only setting around 11 pm. Even then it doesn't actually get dark and the sky remains a navy blue the whole night. By 3am it's getting light again!

It's always lovely being back on familiar ground and seeing old friends and catching up all the news from the last year. We usually stay in the manse on Berneray, but due to it not being fit for habitation this past year, we had been given the manse in Griminsh.

We loved staying on Berneray. The manse was built on the back of the church and if you opened the kitchen door, it would lead straight into the church! The views from the Berneray manse were also spectacular. It was situated up a slight incline from Seal Bay, aptly named due to the huge numbers of seals that would sprawl out on the rocks, basking in the intermittent sunshine. The cacophony of barking that came from the rocks was quite amusing and a delight to hear and to see. They are so cute and would lie on the rocks lazily watching the world go by. I love seals; they remind me of a fat, little white, furry pudding at home called Whisper.

The manse in Griminsh is also lovely. It's a large rambling old building which is beautifully maintained. It has all one needs to live comfortably. It is also much closer to the main town of Balivanich, which is more convenient for grocery shopping and the usual daily needs.

The Islands of North Uist, South Uist, Benbecular and Berneray are joined together by means of huge boulders made into a road called a causeway. They are a feat of modern engineering and make life so much easier than having to sail to every little island as in the old days.

We minister in many of the churches on the Islands. It is so sad to see the numbers of folks attending church diminishing year by year as the aging congregation slowly passes from this life. The younger generation is not found in many of the churches today. Sunday schools are incredibly small and young families attending church are extremely rare. When we first started coming to the Uists around 16 or 17 years ago, many of the churches had strong congregations. The numbers attending the midweek prayer meeting would half fill the church. As the years have gone by we have watched that number dwindle. In spite of the small numbers, we still have wonderful fellowship with those who attend.

We have been given the honour of ministering into many people's lives on a personal basis too, while in the UK. Although the UK is nothing like South Africa and does not have the same level of poverty and deprivation, there are still needs. The needs may not be physical such as hunger or dire need of shelter, although I am sure these do exist; we find the needs are usually in the form of hurt, loneliness, illness or pain. What a privilege to be able to pray for these special people and spend time with them. We humbly thank the Lord for this wonderful opportunity.

On the way to a church, one year, we noticed a tourist taking two dogs for a walk. Not just any two dogs mind you— these were Maltese! So very rare here, you normally see Bichon Fiche's, but not Maltese. I really wanted Gavin to stop but he didn't feel we had enough time to do so. Those two Maltese don't realise their lucky escape. They were nearly attacked by some deranged woman in dire need of a doggie fix!

For a time there was a minister on the Island that owned a little dog named Bruno. I used to love having a cuddle with Bruno, but what really intrigued Gavin and I was Bruno's ability to understand certain words. A delicious treat could be put in front of him and he would be told that the food was bought on credit. Bruno would salivate and stare at the treat but would not touch it! If told that it was OK, the treat was paid for; Bruno would gobble the treat down as quick as a flash.

We often take the Scripture Union class in the Balivanich School. We were so impressed with this school, which to us seemed to have everything that opens and shuts. In the classroom where Scripture Union was held, we noticed on our last trip that the students had been moulding sculptures with Fimo clay. Each child had been given a whole pack of 24 different coloured blocks of Fimo and I know how much one block costs! The funding the schools have in the UK is wonderful to see.

When I think of the little class room in the village of Kwa Lubisi where the Pongola Baptist Church meets, it couldn't be further opposite to what we see here. In Kwa Lubisi the floors are pitted cement, the walls are cracked and dirty, with not one picture or poster. There is one old chalkboard and no chalk. There are no computers, electronic white boards or any books. How vastly different, and how sad, that not all children have equal opportunities. We had a lovely time with the children in Balivanich who were most attentive and intensely interested, especially in our wild game.

We have done many meetings in the schools on the Uists and other Islands. What I particularly enjoy is the lively question and answer sessions after our presentation about the work in South Africa. It usually revolves around the animals we have and our various creepy crawlies. The Labola system, when African men pay for their wives, interests children. Many want to know how many cattle I would be worth!

We have had some lovely meals with our friend Ishie, who organises our accommodation and itinerary for us while we are on the Uists. Ishie and her daughter Donna visit the Kenyan church that is twined with the Griminish and Clachan Churches here on the Island.

Ishie told us that their last visit two years ago was a life changing experience for both her and Donna. We have said the same over many years—one can see pictures of the needs of the people, but that is never enough. A person must personally experience the sights, sounds and smells of Africa and meet her people, to get a glimpse into the complexities and diversity of the problems in Africa.

On a Sunday morning, Gavin would preach in the different Churches and I would do the children's' address. This last year I spoke to the children on fear and how it robs us of peace. This was to tie in with Gavin's sermon later in the service. I had a PowerPoint presentation showing how the Ostrich sticks its head in the sand when frightened, and the children found this hilarious. It is always a great joy for me when the children

Heading for Africa: Ishie and Donna.

react to what is being said to them and seem to find the stories interesting or amusing.

I also have a puppet which is a caricature of a sheep that has big bulging eyes. The sheep has a most interesting name. It is Hooga Woga Zoog Zoog. This never fails to get the children laughing.

Gavin preached on the beatitude "Blessed are the peace makers" and the lack of peace in the world today. It was an inspired message and the Spirit of God was clearly felt moving amongst the congregation. Some folks were in tears. Although I had heard that sermon before, I too was near to tears at the end of it. We are truly humbled by God's grace and mercy.

One Sunday evening we were at the Carinish Free Church of Scotland. The Free Church is more conservative than the

Church of Scotland and I suppose more like our own denomination in South Africa. We do need to be careful of stereotyping people and churches, and that got me thinking about how often we judge people on hearsay or on preconceived ideas. I am so guilty of this and have to truly repent of this annoying habit.

We met Lachie, the Free Church minister, last year. We were expecting a rather formal, serious looking minister to arrive, but what we got instead was—well—Lachie! He and Gavin had so much in common, Lachie being a drummer and Gavin being a piper. More than that, their theology is similar and they are like-minded. Lachie is built a lot like Gavin and this huge man appeared at the Bible study in jeans with shirt and fleece, just not what we were expecting. What a refreshing surprise and what a down to earth—Earthy Christian.

We had an interesting time when we were invited to share in the over-60's yearend party in Griminish. In South Africa, clubs and schools close down at the beginning of December. All year-end functions are at the end of November or early December. Here, that all happens in June, right before the summer holidays.

The over-60's club met at a local restaurant and museum. We had a lovely lunch followed by a tour of the museum. As I'm intensely interested in history, I thoroughly enjoyed the tour. The museum depicted how people lived on the crofts in the past, and the ways they lived off of the land. The disconcerting thing for me was that I remembered using similar implements at my grandmothers' home. We had some of them in our own home when I was a young child. That really made me feel my age.

There was also a wonderful display of artefacts from the First World War. The stark reality of the huge loss of life was made very clear by two photographs. The regiment going off to war had 27 officers and 1,000 men. After their return from the war another photo was taken of the survivors—1 officer and 27 men. I found the numbers shocking and also the eerie coincidence of the number 27. There were 27 officers to start and a total of 27 surviving soldiers. The whole episode was desperately sad and reminds us of the price that was paid that we may live in freedom today.

We have on occasion been invited to participate in the communion service in the Free Church. To us in South Africa, a starting time of 3 pm for a church service is unusual, but it is normal on the Island and all the ladies bring food for a meal afterwards. The denominations here tend to have communion seasons, rather than taking communion on a monthly, bi-monthly or weekly basis as we tend to do.

The whole weekend is set aside to make right with our Lord and to contemplate what we are about to do. This culminates with the Lord's Supper and then there is a service of Thanks Giving afterwards.

A visiting preacher usually does a series of sermons for this special weekend. It's a lovely, thoughtful way of taking communion and we are honoured to be able to share in this holy sacrament with them. As mentioned earlier, there is a veritable feast afterwards. I don't eat fish, but there is usually a huge smoked salmon and also crab salad; not your usual fare at the Church lunches we have attended in the past. A wonderful time of fellowship ensues before we finally make our way back to the manse.

Leaving the Island can sometimes not be as easy as it

sounds. One year we were due to leave the next day, when one of the local ministers asked us to stay an extra day in order to cover for him at the prayer meeting the following evening. He had been called away on unexpected urgent business. Of course we agreed and duly changed our ferry tickets for a sailing two days later.

We took the prayer meeting the following evening and by the time we had finished a huge gale had started blowing. It gathered strength the whole night and by morning all sailings had been cancelled due to adverse weather conditions. Oh dear, this did cause us a problem as we had another meeting on the Isle of Skye that evening. It has been the only meeting that we have had to miss in all our years of travel. Although we did feel awful about not being able to attend, the Islanders are quit used to this type of thing happening. We finally managed to leave the Island the next day. Although a ferry being cancelled has occurred a few times to us over the years this was the only instance of us having to miss a meeting because of it.

On another occasion, our friend Ishie was on board the ferry when it broke down approximately halfway between the two Islands of Berneray and Harris. Poor Ishie never made her meeting as the ferry turned around and limped back into the harbour at Berneray. We had a few anxious days waiting for workers to repair the ferry. We panicked, concerned that we would not get off of the Island in time for our next meeting. Thankfully, the ferry was mended in time and we had a beautiful calm crossing to the Isle of Harris.

While we tensely waited for the ferry to be repaired on

that occasion we took the opportunity to visit with a young American pastor who was completing his Ph.D. at St Andrews University. He was doing a placement in Clachan church for the summer holidays.

It saddens us to hear that people are still not aware of the true state of South Africa. The young pastor told us that to him, his wife and others like them, South Africa is portrayed as a wealthy, beautiful holiday destination. All of this may be true, but there is so much more to South Africa. Tourists need to be warned of the dangers, so that they can be vigilant and careful.

We also met up with the interim moderator for the presbytery of the Island. This lovely, humble man told us of his 5-year experience working in Zimbabwe alongside his wife in an orphanage there. His stories are so similar to ours, and it was so refreshing to hear someone of his calibre concurring with all that we had shared with folks on the Island.

After a tearful goodbye to our friends, and especially to Ishie, we boarded the boat to start the second leg of our journey.

Chapter 13

Revival Country: Lewis

The third leg of our journey takes us to the Isles of Lewis and Harris. The two Islands are very close together and joined by a road. People would not normally know they were crossing from the one Island to the other if it were not for the road sign that says, "Welcome to Lewis" driving north, or "Welcome to Harris" when driving south.

Harris is very different from both Uist and Lewis. It has a beauty that is uniquely its own. We normally talk about beach sand as being silver sand. Here the sand on the beaches is a rich golden colour. Its beauty is far too difficult to describe and no photo could do it justice. There is a fusion of stark granite rocks, glorious golden sand and grass clad mountains all surrounded by turquoise coloured sea. Sheep roam freely and often sleep in the middle of the road as the tar is warmed by the sun. Oh, the joy and blessedness of the gift of sight, to behold such wonders of God's glorious creation.

As one drives further north, finally crossing over onto the Isle of Lewis, the scenery and feel of the place changes. Because no trees used to grow on Lewis, one can see for literally miles in any direction. I remember the first time we came to Lewis, crossing the moors was quite a frightening experience for me because I felt like a tiny speck in the huge cosmos, and that thoroughly intimidated me. Subsequently, I have gotten used to it.

Although Harris is barren, some individuals on Lewis have tried planting trees in their gardens recently. One sees a few brave little saplings bent almost at a 90 degree angle from the wind desperately trying to grow strong and tall.

Lewis holds a very special place in my heart, especially the town of Barvis, as it was here in the Church of Scotland where the revival of 1949-1953 started. The Lord used a man, Duncan Campbell, to bring revival to the Island. Many wonderful and extra ordinary events happened during that time and are still spoken of today. Barvis Church of Scotland was the very first church that Gavin preached in on the Western Isles.

We have the privilege of knowing the very first convert from that revival—Rev John Murdo Smith. He is well into his 80's now, but something extraordinarily holy still lingers in his presence. To sit at his feet and learn from him is of great benefit and joy. He and his wife, Margaret, are an inspiration to us and we would hope to leave a legacy such as theirs.

Gavin and I had always wanted to come to Lewis to see first-hand where the Revival had begun. In 1997, we had an opportunity for the first time, to come up to Lewis for a few days. We had very little finance, and not being able to afford accommodation, we parked our little car in the local caravan park just outside of Stornoway and slept in the car.

Since our luggage takes up not only the boot but the whole back seat as well, we had to sleep sitting up straight and it was a very uncomfortable, cold, long night. The next morning we went to the town of Barvis to see the Church where the Spirit of God had first come down.

While still on mainland Scotland, one of our friends, after hearing of our intention to visit the Island, asked us to pass their greetings on to the local Minister. The manse is next to the church so we knocked on the door ready to deliver the message entrusted to us.

Ivor MacDonald (the minister at that time) answered the door and after hearing the message invited us in for a cup of tea. What was intended to be a quick "cuppa" turned into a four hour time of sharing and wonderful fellowship. We had so much in common and became firm and fast friends from that day. After our visit, Ivor and his wife Rosemary, inquired as to our accommodation. Too embarrassed to say that we were sleeping in our car at the caravan site we just replied, "Oh, we are staying in Stornoway." They promptly insisted that we move in with them for the duration of our stay. Once again our Jehovah Jireh provided through His people.

To this day we are friends with Ivor and Rosemary, visiting them each year. Ivor was responsible for opening the doors of the Church of Scotland to us on the Island. He started arranging our itinerary each year, and did so faithfully until he was called to the Church of Scotland in Staffin on the Isle of Skye. Ivor is now the minister of The Free Church of Scotland in Coatbridge, where he still very graciously allows us to share about the work in South Africa with the folks in his charge.

Ivor MacDonald who introduced us to Lewis.

It is an enormous pity that now, some 60 years later, the lingering presence of holiness that was on the Island is, in general, disappearing. As commercialism and materialism have made their home here, so the holy presence of God has quietly and benignly withdrawn. When we first visited Lewis in the mid 1990's the feeling of the place was very different from what it is today. Everyone knew then, what it meant to be a Christian, even if you weren't one. Sundays were holy days with absolutely nothing open, even the airport and ferry terminals being closed. One didn't drive on a Sunday and the only activity was going to church. Sadly, that has all been done away with over the last twenty years. Now, Sunday is still markedly different from other days, but the ferry and airports operate, and a few shops and garages are open too. One sees many more cars on the road. Now even washing is hung out on the Sabbath.

Presently, when on Lewis we are hosted by two dear friends, Pam and Gary. We met Pam through her son who used to attend the same Bible Study as us in South Africa. Pam and Gary attend the more conservative of the denominations on the Island. We do sometimes find the lifestyle a little challenging. No TV, radio, newspapers and no magazines. No jeans or slacks, only skirts for ladies and hats are an absolute must for all church related functions. There are few mirrors in the house and this makes me aware of how vain I am with my need to have a mirror to apply makeup and see if my buttons are fastened. I have learned much from these dear folks since there is just so much of the world still in me.

On one of our very rare free Sunday evenings, we went along with Pam and Gary to the Free Church Continuing. (With obligatory hat firmly stuck on my head!) I did feel rather conspicuous as most of the ladies were either in black or navy and here I was in my bright scarlet jacket! No matter, the people were very friendly.

After the service, the minister, Greg, invited us over to the manse for tea. What a blessed time of fellowship we had together. Once again we found so much common ground. That is the joy of the mutual bond that ties Christians together. Greg actually did his high schooling in the Transkei while his folks were on a mission station there. He has a good knowledge and understanding of South Africa and her unique problems and challenges.

One year we drove to the Butt of Lewis near the lighthouse

for a walk. A friend had asked me to find her a heart shaped stone so I had thought that this was probably the best place to look for one. As Gavin is now unable to walk any length of distance, he sat in the car and let me walk the cliffs within sight of him, of course. Oh, what a blessed time of being alone with my God!

As I wondered around the cliffs, taking in the beauty that surrounded me, I had an intense experience of our precious Lord. As I looked out across the wide expanse of ocean curtained by rugged cliffs, I felt the Lord ask me the very question He had asked the disciple Peter all those years ago: "Peter, do you love me more than all these?"

I started crying as I felt that question "Des, do you love me more than all these?" Now "these", being the things, that are most precious to me, my most beloved treasures, whether loved ones or things.

Crying, I fell to my knees, "Lord," I cried, "You know my heart." Then I thought of the man, who after asking Jesus to heal his servant, Jesus asked him if he believed that He could heal him, the man cried, "Lord, I believe, help my unbelief". I sobbed, "Lord, I do love you more than these, help me to love you more than these".

As I stood up, I looked to the ground and at my feet was a heart shaped stone. What gentle love our Saviour has for us and how precious, is that relationship with Him!

Martin's Memorial Church of Scotland in the town of Stornoway is one of our longest supporting churches, going way back to the mid to the late 1990's. Tommy MacNeil, the current minister, is rapidly gaining a reputation as a conference speaker.

As we look back over the years, we have watched a number of young men go into the ministry. It has been a delight for us to watch them mature into their respective charges. While participating in open air meetings in the town of Stornoway, Tommy would sing in the music group with us. We watched him grow from a young probationer at Martin's Memorial to becoming the minister at Barvis Church of Scotland. Now he has come full circle, back to Martin's Memorial as the minister.

Rev Iain Murdo MacDonald has been a faithful friend and supporter for many years. Iain is another minister on the Island and he mentioned to his congregation that he has lost count of the number of years we have been coming to his church. He remembered what I had not known. That is, he was present at the open air meeting years ago, when we were taking the service and a drunk came up to the microphone and started shouting and swearing over Gavin as he was preaching. Gavin reached out his hand and prayed quietly that the Lord would shut the man's mouth. As quickly as the drunk had started shouting, he quietly shut his mouth and moved away. I did not know that Iain Murdo was there that day.

Iain Murdo has accepted a call to Tarbet and the congregation in Ness is grieving for him. The ladies at Ness always make a huge fuss over us both, and we are touched by their genuine love and concern for our well-being.

We also have meetings in the APC Church in Stornoway. The folks in the APC are good friends, us having shared in that church on an annual basis for many years. Our association with the APC started in the 1990's and on our first visit to

Gavin preaching and playing pipes at the open air service in Stornoway.

that church we were invited to the ministers' house for a meal before the service.

We were both aware that he wanted to make sure that we were "theologically sound" before letting us loose on his congregation. The questions began to flow at the table while eating. Gavin dutifully answered the inquiries on our stance on various issues, and in the course of the conversation he mentioned another dear friend, David Carmichael. David has been a mentor to Gavin and an inspiration to us both.

The minister stopped Gavin in midsentence and asked "Do you preach in David's church?" "Yes, every year" answered Gavin. "Oh well, that's good enough for me," he said and all questioning came to an abrupt end.

Every year on one of the Sundays that we are on Lewis we drive the roughly three hour trip down to Leverburgh, on Harris for both the morning and evening services. This past year we met the new minister and his wife, shared lunch with them and spent the afternoon together. As there are so many linked charges, David (the minister) went off to preach in Manish and Gavin and I went on our own for Gavin to preach in Scarista. Both the morning and evening services went very well and once again we feel so humbled by God's goodness and peoples' kindness. It was nearly midnight by the time we finally arrived back in Ness and after an 8 am start it had been a long day indeed.

Leaving the Isle of Lewis can be a logistical nightmare. The problem is that we have to leave Ness at 5 am. We have to be at the ferry terminal by 6 am as the boat to Ullapool leaves at 7 am. We arrive in Ullapool around 11 am, then, it's a three and a half hour drive up to Gills Bay from where we catch a ferry at 4 pm to Orkney, arriving at 5.30 pm. So, you can see why I need to pack up and load as much as possible the day before.

Often we have quite a lot of rain so I have to wait for the rain to stop before I could start loading the car. I often feel it would be better to load in the rain as after the showers the midges come out. These are not like our harmless little miggies in South Africa. These terrorists have horned Viking helmets with special drills that pack a punch! Just joking, but that's what it feels like. Their bite is really nasty, leaving something akin to our mosquito bite, just a little

smaller. Sometimes these bites become infected for whatever reason and can make some nasty sores. I was almost
devoured by these vile little monsters. They get in under your
clothing, down behind your collar and onto your back. Your
hair gets full of them and your whole face stings. It can be a
most wretched experience. Usually, after most of the packing
is done, I concede defeat to a worthy opponent and find shelter indoors.

After completing all the meetings on Lewis, we have a tremendous sense of peace and fulfilment, although it is still a
wrench to leave this very special place that has such a Godly
history. We say our fond farewells to our hosts the night before
and after getting up at 4 am the next morning quietly creep out
of the house to start the long day ahead of us.

Chapter 14

Sailing the High Seas: Orkney and Westray

I could never explain how utterly exhausting it is to travel the huge distances we must often transverse. The ferry crossing from the Isle of Lewis, back to mainland Scotland is not a bad journey at all. Often thick fog and mist accompanies us for the whole journey and one hears the sorrowful moan of the foghorn calling out in the cold white morning.

The drive all the way to the very northerly tip of Scotland, at John O'Groats, is very pleasant. The heather is just starting to bloom at this time of the year, and although the landscape is not yet fully purple, there are bursts of this beautiful little flower all over the hills giving them a polka dot look. The sky can be clear and the sea a beautiful deep blue, so a lovely drive up, with me just enjoying the backdrop of God's glorious handiwork.

One year before crossing to Orkney, we decided to take the

opportunity of a boat ride around the coast adjacent to John 'O Groats. Much marine life can be seen, bird life as well and of course, my favourite—seals.

We were required to don huge waterproof jackets called oil skins, and on top of these we had lifejackets tied to our bodies. Looking and feeling strange and cumbersome, we finally climbed aboard the vessel for our sightseeing tour. We had only just left the harbour when the engine cut out which made the two gentlemen who were our guides immediately focus all their attention on the problem. The boat in the meantime was at the mercy of the tides and bobbed up and down furiously being tossed this way and that.

So, focused on the task at hand, the two guides did not notice what we had, that we were drifting at some speed straight towards an outcrop of jagged rocks. We were becoming alarmed when at the last minute one of the guides looked up and saw the imminent danger. They both immediately stopped what they were doing and furiously steered the boat away from the rocks.

It was a slow and laborious row back to the mainland without us ever catching even a glimpse of my beloved seals.

The ferry crossing from mainland Scotland across to Orkney can be treacherous. We fear this crossing as the Pentland Firth is known as one of the most dangerous stretches of water in the world. The under currents here are extremely strong and the boat normally pitches in all directions making one very aware of one's own mortality.

One year we sailed in a Gale Force 10 winds and I would rather not do that again. The tables and chairs on the boat are fastened to the floor on long strips of wire. As the boat would ascend the huge wave the chairs would slide to one side of the boat as far as the wire would let them. Once the boat crested the wave, the vessel would totter there for a moment before being plunged down the other side of the wave. We would count, one, one thousand, two, one thousand until at least five or six one thousand when we would finally hit the bottom of the wave and the whole boat would crash and shudder, sending chairs and tables, scurrying in the opposite direction. It is not a journey I would ever want to repeat!

Thankfully, we had a good crossing this year and although utterly exhausted by this time, arrived safely in St Margaret's Hope around 6 pm Monday evening. Some very kind folks from the Kirkwall Baptist Church put us up for the night. After dinner and a short visit we finally collapsed into bed.

Leaving St Margaret's Hope the next morning we had to drive from the Island of South Ronaldsay, across the Island of Burra and onto the Mainland of Orkney. The largest Island of the Orkney's is called "Mainland". These Islands are connected through means of large causeways as I mentioned on other Islands. The causeways were built by Italian prisoners during World War II and there is a little Italian Chapel on Burra which they constructed and used for worship during their imprisonment here. At one point at Scappa Flow, wrecks from ships sunken during that war are clearly visible. Their rusted masts rise forlornly out from the murky waters below.

The Northern Isles are very different from the Western Isles. The Western Isles have mountains and a rocky terrain, while the Northern Isles have gentle sloping hills and grassy plains. There are many more farms here and although the scenery is less dramatic, it's still very beautiful.

Last year as it was a lovely day with no wind, the ocean was beautifully calm, so we decided not to take our sea sick tablets for the crossing from mainland Orkney to the Isle of Westray. The crossing takes around one and a half hours and about a half an hour into the journey the boat started to pitch and roll. Two opposing tides were coming in from different directions and although the sea looked calm and there was no wind, it was one of the most awful sea journeys we have ever experienced. Gavin says that I was positively grey by the time we landed. I didn't seem to get over that awful nausea the rest of the day. Gavin recovered the moment our feet touched dry ground.

We stayed with John and Violet who have been friends of ours for years now. It was a lovely reunion and the rest of the day was spent in sweet fellowship and the usual unpacking. The next morning the pain in my head woke me up. I had a severe migraine attack, probably triggered by over tiredness and excessive travelling. On top of that I had vertigo and I couldn't even lift my head off the pillow.

I was diagnosed with Meniere's disease but in addition to that it was discovered upon our return to South Africa that I actually had a virus that attacked my cochlea which has left me with permanent hearing loss and balance difficulties.

That evening we had a missions meeting and I knew that if I didn't attend, there would be supporters that I would not get another opportunity to see before we left Westray. After staying in bed the whole day, and although still extremely "fragile" and not steady on my feet at all, I managed to attend the meeting and do my part of the presentation. I'm so glad that I did attend as it was delightful to see everyone once again.

There is one precious soul here on Westray to whom I owe a huge debt of gratitude. Little Annie, as she is known, took a vivid interest in Deanne when she was so desperately ill a few years ago. Little Annie prayed faithfully and daily for my child, and I will forever be grateful.

The next day John and Violet took us for a tour around the Island—not that we haven't done this before—we have done it many times. But on a small island the places to visit are rather limited. We went to the airfield, which is interesting because it's so tiny. The sign on the terminal building door reads "Passengers to book in 10 minutes before departure. Beware of propellers". If only that was the same in other airports. From the terminal building one can see the airstrip on Papa Westray which is the little Island just north of Westray. The shortest flight in the world is from Westray to Papa Westray and lasts 2 minutes.

We also went to see the Holmy sheep. These sheep are unique in that they only eat seaweed; this affects the taste of the meat which is very distinctive. The meat is considered a delicacy and is served in exclusive restaurants and five star hotels.

We then went for a "haf yok"—the Orkadian for a tea break. We had bere bannocks and fatty cutties, both delicious and exclusive to the Orkneys.

After sad farewells once again we sailed back to Mainland Orkney. Upon arriving after an uneventful journey we took a

John and Violet who all but adopted us on Westray.

drive to Scarra Brae. I have always been fascinated with history and this place intrigues me. According to archaeology and carbon dating, this village, which was uncovered after a very bad storm a couple of years ago, is thought to be about 7,000 years old. For those of us who hold a young earth viewpoint, this village then, would have been built not very long after the flood. It's amazing to see how they had beds, shelves and toilets all made from stone. As King Solomon said, "There is nothing new under the sun"—no indeed, it's all been done before us!

On our first visit to Orkney, we stayed with David and Jacqueline, who are now firm friends. Usually, as it was in this case, when meeting strangers for the first time, conversation can be a bit stilted. Both David and Jacqueline are quiet, gentle souls and while making conversation we enquired about their family.

David brought out a photograph album and upon opening the book, on the front page was a very familiar face. Both Gavin and I exclaimed together, "We know him!" David answered with a look of amazement on his face, "That's my Dad!" The Lord has his people all across the world, and how these threads come together without us ever realising it. It was wonderful to learn of this connection. We had been sharing in Carrubbers church in Edinburgh for many years and David's dad, Eric, is an elder in that church. Having common ground, the ice was broken and we had a lovely visit which cemented our relationship.

Another year, while visiting with Jacqueline and David, Jacqueline told us that her sister Heather was the resident organist at the huge Cathedral in Kirkwall.

The St Magnus Cathedral is the biggest in the highlands and has a wonderful history and legend that goes with it. It is told that the two Earls of Orkney, Hakon and Magnus who ruled in the 12th century, were cousins, and unfortunately the joint rule didn't last long. After some treachery Magnus was captured by Hakon and ordered to be executed. According to the sagas that have been written about this episode, Magnus meekly agreed to his fate. He told his executioner that those ordering his death were sinning more than the one carrying out the deed. Magnus was canonised some years later and the Cathedral was built in honour of his memory. During renovations of the Cathedral in 1919 a box with bones was discovered, which some believe are Magnus's remains. Whether fact or fiction, the cathedral is a most impressive building and one can feel the history seeping from the stones.

Heather knew of Gavin's love of playing the bagpipes and very kindly offered to accompany him on the huge pipe organ in the Cathedral. Gavin, dressed in his kilt, played the most befitting hymn sung to the tune of "Highland Cathedral" while Heather skilfully played the wonderful big old organ. They produced, between the two of them, the most beautiful music. Many tourists came streaming into the Church, to listen to the unique Scottish harmony, taking photographs and videos with their mobile phones. We teased Gavin saying he mustn't speak because if the tourists heard a South African accent instead of a Scottish one, the whole allusion would be broken!

This year's services on Orkney once again were truly blessed. Gavin preached in the Kirkwall Baptist Church on "Abraham—the father of a nation". He had many compliments after the service which encouraged him enormously. At the evening service we presented our missions feedback and it was a special time of sharing with the body of Christ. We did have a power cut during the service though, but we continued in the dark as though nothing was wrong and eventually the electricity was restored.

After the service we were due to catch the boat to Shetland. Not having had dinner, we had no choice but to go into the Chinese takeaway for food. Gavin, in a teasing mood, decided to play a little joke on the assistants inside. From his years in China, he had learned that the Chinese liked their food very fresh and many restaurants have fresh fish in tanks for this purpose. Customers choose their fish from the tank which would then be caught and cooked. Gavin walked into the fast food restaurant and there was a fish tank with gold fish swimming around. When asked what he wanted to order, he walked over to the fish tank and pointed to the largest of the goldfish saying "That one—I want that one." The poor Chinese man nearly had an apoplexy gesturing with his hands and saying over and over again "No eaty, no eaty!"

I was still unwell and fearful of the long sea journey; the boat leaving at 11.30 pm, arriving in Shetland at 7 am the next morning. We did not have a cabin since they are extremely expensive. The doctor recommended I fly and Gavin take the car, but that not being an option, the next best is to be able to lie down flat. All cabins were fully booked so our next option was a "sleeping pod". This is a glorified reclining chair supplied with a small pillow and blanket. I took the tablets I was given to increase the blood flow to my ears, a seasick tablet and a sleeping tablet. Probably over the top—but I really didn't want a repeat of the past week. The tablets knocked me out completely and I have no memory of the journey at all. I awoke when we docked in Lerwick, and nearly 12 hours later still felt drugged, so probably over did it, but at least I survived the trip.

Chapter 15

Shetland Safari

Some very kind folks from the United Free Church in Cunningsburgh, Malcolm and Liz, allow us the use of their home on Shetland while they are away on holiday. On our first visit to their home they asked us to please take care of their cat, "Mr Puss". Although I am an animal lover, cats are not exactly my favourite creatures. My main objection is their killing of other small animals.

Liz very kindly left us two pages of notes with instructions of how to use various appliances in the house and how to care for Mr Puss. One of her comments was that Mr Puss likes to bring half-eaten bunny rabbits into the house. This nearly freaked me out! I spent the whole week over feeding poor old Mr Puss making sure that he was so well fed that he didn't feel the need to go hunting! So far each time that we have stayed in Malcolm and Liz's beautiful home Mr Puss has been an extremely well behaved kitty and we are actually forming a good friendship—cat and I.

After staying with folks for so much of the time it is lovely being on our own and having a measure of privacy again, eating what we want, when we want, and how much we want.

We have been most graciously received on Shetland, and all the meetings thus far have been good ones. My only real difficulty in these meetings is the accent of the people. I can cope with Doric, Orkadian and Glaswegian but Shetlander might as well be Martian. Most vowels are exchanged for a U (as in "UP") so the word "walk" for instance comes out as "WUK". Their own words for certain things just adds to the confusion. The "do not litter" signs read "DUNNA CHUCK BRUCK". Small or tiny is said to be "PEERIE". All people not native to the Shetlands are called "SOOTHERS" because visitors come from the south as the boat comes into Lerwick from that direction. I'm sure you will understand when I say that at times the conversation goes right over my head.

Shetland, as with the other Isles, is different once again and has a beauty that is unique to it. It is green with gentle rolling hills clothed in heather and a variety of little yellow and white flowers. There are lots of Shetland ponies that graze lazily on the hills, and there are also plenty of sheep.

Very few trees grow due to the amount of wind that blows. Shetland is booming because of the oil industry and jobs are very easily come by. Accommodation is scarce as every B&B and hotel is filled to capacity with migrant workers. Things became so critical that huge floating blocks of flats have been brought in from Europe. They are extremely ugly looking beasts that sit tied up on the pier, but they do serve a very practical purpose and alleviate a real problem.

Being so far north makes things a little strange for us. We are on the same latitude as Moscow and are wedged between Norway and Iceland. Although it is already a month past the summer solstice, the sun still does not truly set. It just dips beyond the horizon and there is a glow there the whole night and it just doesn't get dark. Apparently just the opposite is true in winter with very little daylight, and people often suffer from Seasonal Affective Disorder, commonly known as SAD. This is due to a lack of light and/or sunshine.

One can understand why in times past there were pagan festivals to appease the gods, to make sure the sun returned in summer. A recent festival though, is the Up Helly Aa festival. I was fortunate enough to attend a mini-Up Helly Aa Festival on Westray last year, but would dearly love to attend "the real thing". It all culminates in the burning of a Viking ship. It's now of course, just a bit of fun and no one takes it seriously.

Shetland has a lot of Norse culture left over from the past when the Islands belonged to Norway. This is evident in the very strange place names that I wouldn't even hazard a guess how to pronounce. Most sign boards with the town's name on it, has underneath "The old Norse for... (then whatever it means). For example, Lerwick is the Old Norse for "Muddy Bay". The names can be rather strange and funny to us as outsiders. We are staying in Airthsetter, which is not bad if you consider that we are between the villages of Quarff and Wilhoull. Some locals we have met consider themselves to be more Norse than Scottish and all the tourist shops have Viking helmets and mini-Viking ships for sale.

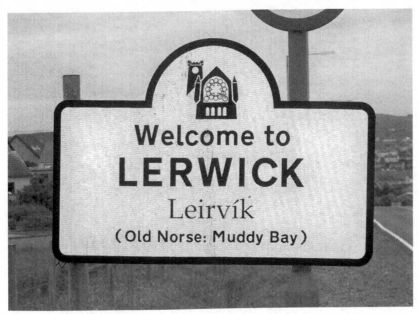

A road sign on Shetland.

After a particularly busy and draining Sunday, filled with meetings and ministry we took Monday off to relax. I could see across the bay to a beautiful lighthouse from the local supermarket where we were doing some grocery shopping. I suggested to Gavin that we take a drive there, even though the weather was bad. With nothing else to do we headed off in that direction.

An hour and a half later we were still looking for the road to the lighthouse when the "penny finally dropped" and I realised that in fact the lighthouse was on another Island and that a body of water separated us from it. How stupid I felt! Needless to say, we were not going to cross to the Island of Burrsay on a ferry in such foul weather, so decided instead to drive to the west of the island. We crossed a couple of causeways, covered a couple of the smaller islands, and eventually had a reasonable morning.

We have so many friends on the Island that we have many dinners out with folks and have many interesting evenings. We are often out every night for nearly the entire duration of our stay in Shetland. I have found it quite tiring, too many late nights and too much rich food do not make a good combination!

On one trip we had been stuck indoors during the day most of the week, but had decided to go out later that day. I just hoped the fog and mist would lift. There had been very heavy fog for a few days and it was so bad that one could not see across the road. The airport was closed, and one of our visitors told us that the airport better be open the next day. He was getting married on the week end and had been trapped on the Island because of the fog.

Although warm, the mist and fog just wouldn't clear. We drove to the Sumborugh Lighthouse where we were told some spectacular views are to be seen. Although we did find it interesting, the mist was so thick that all we could really make out was up to a few feet in front of us. The cliffs were very dramatic and I could just imagine the beauty of the place on a clear day. We saw hundreds of Puffins and I was fortunate enough to be able to get really near one and take a close up photo.

To get to Sumborough Lighthouse, one passes the airport and actually has to drive across the run way. It was the strangest experience. Although I took photos, they are not descriptive enough to really illustrate just how unusual this is. The end of the runway is a sheer drop off the cliffs and into the sea. Very different, indeed.

The next day the mist had lifted and it was a glorious day. Trust us to go to the lighthouse in the mist and then the very next day it was so clear, you could see for miles. I went for a walk along the cliffs and took some photos. It was really stunning.

A few years ago, there was a so-called heat wave here. I say so-called because coming from South Africa, where temperatures of thirty five degrees Celsius are the norm in summer, we do not find Shetland warm. Some older folks were forced to leave the Island for a while seeking cooler temperatures and the locals were really struggling with the heat. The top temperature during that heat wave was around twenty degrees and my jersey was still a permanent fixture on my body.

Our last Sunday on Shetland a few years ago was a very eventful day. Gavin was due to preach at the Dunrossness Baptist Church and we were also going to share about the work in South Africa. It was a lovely drive to the church and the weather was glorious by Shetland standards.

To get to the church, one has to turn off of the main road onto a smaller road for a short while. As we turned, the car made a loud "CLANK" and Gavin couldn't change gears. "The gear box has broken!" cried Gavin.

We pulled over to the side of the road. While Gavin stayed with the car, I walked the rest of the way to the church. I kept praying, "Thank you Lord, that it's not raining, there are no gales blowing and the midges are not out. Things could be a lot worse!"

Thankfully, we had left in good time, so I arrived at the church with plenty of time to spare. The minister, Ian, was already there and it was a huge relief to explain the problem to him. He immediately found someone who was prepared to fetch Gavin and our equipment.

When Gavin arrived, we were each given a small microphone to attach to our clothing, which we duly did. Just before the service started, I decided to pop into the Ladies bathroom. Forgetting about the microphone attached to the waistband of my skirt, it unattached itself and went hurtling across the bathroom floor and shattered into tiny pieces. I was absolutely mortified!

While gathering up the broken bits of microphone, I noticed the zip on my skirt was also undone. Not for anything in the world would the zip close. Somehow it too had been damaged. Now on top of everything else, I had a gaping hole in my skirt and my under clothing was clearly visible to all.

In utter embarrassment I humbly took what remained of the microphone to Ian and then still had to ask if he had a safety pin that I could use. He was most understanding and found the first aid kit, in which was a huge safety pin, approximately the size of the old fashioned nappy pin. This was all that was available so my skirt was held together with a huge silver appendage and I was given a handheld microphone instead. Notwithstanding these difficulties, the meeting went well and folks were welcoming and friendly. One couple in the congregation kindly offered us the use of their car so that we could attend another meeting later that evening.

We were due to have lunch with Ian and Morag so we went home with them and Ian phoned the AA to come and fetch our vehicle. We watched forlornly as our car was towed away to Lerwick. It was most disconcerting as we were booked on the ferry for the next evenings' sailing back to Orkney. There is a sailing every second night and if we changed our sailing for a later one, we would miss our next scheduled meeting. We explained our fears to Ian, expressing the need for the vehicle to be fixed before 5 pm the next day. He smiled broadly and said to leave it to him as his friend was the mechanic at the garage. Early the next morning, Ian fetched Gavin and the two of them went to the garage to see what could be arranged. When all was said and done, our car was fixed by mid-afternoon and we were able to pack up and made the ferry with fifteen minutes to spare.

Friends in deed: Ian and Morag.

Because we were disembarking in Kirkwall on Orkney at midnight, we originally did not think it necessary to book a sleeping pod to lie down. However, because of me being diagnosed with Meniere's disease we were having second thoughts about the wisdom of our decision. We enquired about sleeping pods as soon as we boarded but were informed that every single cabin, every sleeping pod and even every reclining chair was booked. The only place for people who had not booked anything was to sit in the bars or the coffee lounges. We have done this many times in the past and it has never been a problem; it was just because of my health that we were now slightly concerned. So, there being nothing we could do, we headed for one of the coffee bar lounges where we were able to sit.

Just after the boat left the harbour, one of the crew members came into the lounge and removed the "reserved" stickers from four of the reclining chairs. I'm not one for quick thinking or quick actions, but I flew off of my chair, threw my handbag on one of the recliners and plopped down on the other.

There were many locals hanging around who obviously knew of this procedure, where if there are cancellations or "no shows", then the seats are available on a first-come, first-served basis. There is a scramble to see who can get to the seats first. I obviously didn't know any of this and am just so grateful because only the Lord could have made me move so fast. Although we hadn't booked or paid for seats, we had reasonably comfortable chairs that reclined a bit and it was so much better than sitting in the café bar for 6 hours.

As I reclined on a comfortable chair and laid my head back, I thought of the scripture that tells us of Jesus having no place to lay his head. However, once again He had provided a place for me to lay mine. How good our God is! He truly does supply all our needs.

We arrived back in Orkney around midnight and made our way to a previously booked B&B. We wouldn't normally pay for a B&B but didn't feel that we could arrive at someone's house in the middle of night, sleep for a few hours, then leave early the next morning. It would be "using" our friends, so we decided just pay the bill and have some rest in a B&B.

We left early Tuesday morning and drove to St Margaret's Hope to catch the ferry back to mainland Scotland. The crossing was quite unpleasant with the Pentland Firth playing her usual game of conflicting tides pulling against each other. Arriving in Gill's Bay, looking and feeling rather "green," we were glad to place our feet on solid ground once more.

Chapter 16

Open Your Ears and Listen! Keswick

A couple of years ago, winter had set in unusually early and when we landed at Gills Bay on the north coast of main land Scotland, it was snowing very heavily. Coming from South Africa, which hardly ever sees snow; this was a unique experience for us. It was difficult to see while driving, as the snow was being swept by the wind and it was creating an optical illusion. I felt as though I was in a revolving tunnel, it was one of the strangest experiences I have had.

After a short while we realised that it was simply too dangerous to continue and decided to find a place to stay for the night. We pulled into a quaint little hotel in a charming village and with gratitude enjoyed warmth and shelter for the night. The next morning when we tried to open our car doors, everything was frozen shut and we had to wait for the car to thaw before we could continue with our journey. As I mentioned earlier, coming from South Africa, we were not used to these situations and found them to be disruptive and stressful. Thankfully we have adjusted over the years and we do tend to try and do most of our travelling in Scotland during the summer months.

The drive down to Dornoch is beautiful whatever the weather. Even when dull and raining most of the way, it does not detract from the beauty of this part of the world. When the heather finally blooms the hills are just covered in purple and green. The rivers flow fast and furious because of the rain and there are mini waterfalls running right next to the road. It is truly charming.

We stay with our friend Barrie for two nights and have a meeting at the Dornoch Christian Fellowship each year. Once again it is just lovely to see familiar faces and reacquaint ourselves with many folks.

It's about a 3 hour drive, from Dornoch to Buckie but a very pleasant one. One passes many barley fields, their golden hue crying out to the fact that they are ready for harvest. The barley is destined for the many malt whiskey distilleries that are dotted around the area. Many famous distilleries are up here, names like Chever's Regal, Inchgower and Glenmorangie. But I look at these fields of barley and wonder how much sadness they are likely to bring, how many headaches and hangovers, how much unhappiness, anger and strife will result from these beautiful golden fields. What a shame and a pity that God's goodness and provision can be so poorly used.

We always stay with Graeme and Ann when in this part of the country. Dear old friends of long standing who put up

Graeme and Ann, Rob and Edna at our stall at Buckie.

with us each and every year while we attend the Keswick in Buckie Convention.

This Christian Convention has been a blessing and delight over the years. The Lord has used Keswick in Buckie to open many doors to various churches for us. We have met many outstanding preachers and wonderful Christian ministers who have often then invited us to come and minister to their respective congregations. This has always been a joy for us to do and accept it as a huge privilege and blessing.

We have a Missionary stand at the convention where folks can come and chat to us. We have display boards with photographs of South Africa and information leaflets.

I also make greetings cards which are slightly different from

My handmade Christian greetings cards for sale.

the norm and are very popular. As cards with truly Christian verses are getting harder to find, these cards serve a purpose for those who like to bless their Christian family and friends with something sincerely meaningful and not frivolous.

The card making started a few years ago as a creative outlet when I was forced to stop making my beloved bears. I used to make handmade Mohair teddy bears which brought me much satisfaction. While in the UK, Gavin would spend many hours working on sermon preparation and this left me with some spare hours and I sorely needed to keep busy. As I am a child at heart and love all things cute, soft and furry; making teddy bears was pure enchantment.

After years of this activity the Rheumatoid Arthritis in my gnarled fingers and hands made it almost impossible to push a needle through the plush fur. With great sadness I finally realised that the teddy bear making days were over and was at a loss as how to fill the empty space they left in my life. A close friend suggested that I start making greetings cards. I originally scoffed at the idea thinking that no one would be interested in buying them as the market is flooded with cards of all kinds.

Nevertheless, as I started to experiment, I found enjoyment in working with paper, which was so much easier than working with fur and a lot less messy. To my astonishment people started buying the cards and now over the years I have gained quite a reputation for my cards. The sale of these is something of a blessing to us each year. It is operated on an "honesty box" system where people choose the cards they want and the monies are placed in a tin on the table. This had worked for years with never a problem until last year, we found about half of the stock of cards gone but just one pound in the tin. What a shame that even at a Christian Convention, the ways of the world are starting to creep in. Nonetheless, the cards are a small source of income which Gavin and I use mainly towards our travelling costs.

It is a tremendous pleasure for me, to this day, to walk into a home and find one of my beloved bears sitting in a corner, near a fireplace or a staircase landing, or even on a bed.

Just before Keswick starts I always have a sense of standing on a precipice of a week filled with expectation and excitement. I am always eager to hear God's word being preached by faithful men who have been anointed with the gift of expounding His Holy word. I reverently await for God's still small voice to speak to me and teach me all that He would have me know.

It's a busy week and an exhausting one but one that I grasp with both hands. It's an awesome privilege to be able to sit under such teaching.

We have experienced cold, wet conventions and we have had hot humid conventions. I remember one particular convention where even by South African standards it was hot. We are used to a dry heat at home, so the humidity here plays a huge factor in making us uncomfortable.

As parking can be a problem at times during the convention, we decided that particular day to walk to the church. We passed rows of parked cars and came across one car that had a gorgeous little dog inside. What upset us both was that all the windows were closed and this poor little mite was panting and puffing.

I was horrified at what I saw and not knowing what to do we took down the registration of the vehicle. We asked the organisers of the convention to announce the registration number in the hope of rescuing the poor suffering creature. No one came forward and I was so terribly upset that I couldn't concentrate on what was being taught that morning. I just kept praying over and over again that the Lord would intervene on behalf of one of His helpless little creatures.

As soon as the meeting was over, we rushed outside to check on the dog, only to find that God in His great mercy had sent the "harr". Harr is the local name for the thick cool mist that rolls in off the ocean. The temperatures had dropped dramatically and the sweet little animal was sitting contentedly on the back ledge of the car, watching the world go by!

We stayed in various places in the years before Ann and Graeme hosted us. One year we were housed in a caravan and early one morning I was awakened with heavy knocking on the caravan. I flew out of bed to answer the door wondering who on earth would need us at such an unearthly hour. Upon opening the caravan door, there was no one in sight. Slightly perplexed and a little miffed I went back to bed. I had no sooner snuggled down under the covers when the awful knocking resumed! More reluctantly this time, I got out of bed and answered the door. Yet again there was no one in sight. Feeling angrier by the minute, thinking there were pranksters about, I resolved to catch them out. Hiding behind the door of the caravan I had a clear view of anyone walking up to the door. Then again the loud knocking started, but lo and behold there was no one at the door! Through thorough investigation, I later discovered that water, from the rain or morning dew, collected in the ridges of the caravan roof and the sea gulls would land on the roof to drink the water. The loud knocking was made by their beaks hitting the roof while drinking!

There is no meeting on the Sunday morning of the convention so everyone is free to go to a church of their choosing. The very first year we attended the convention, we were still very unfamiliar with the churches in the area and just picked one to attend that first Sunday morning.

I will never forget walking into the church and nearly burst out laughing at the music that the man seated at the organ was playing. It sounded as though we were at fair ground not a holy place of worship. That set the mood for the whole service which we sat uncomfortably through.

We were finally called up to the altar rail to partake of the communion and there were two steps leading to the rail. On the way back to my seat I forgot about the two steps and stepping into midair, took a tumble down the steps landing with a loud thump on my rear end with my skirt up around my shoulders. With face burning a bright red, I sheepishly scurried back to my seat wishing the ground would swallow me up.

One year our good friend, Tommy, the minister in the Stornoway Church of Scotland, was one of the speakers. Tommy preached on "Revival" and no one better qualified to do so, as Tommy pastored the Barvis Church where the Lewis revival broke out 60 years ago. Tommy knows many of the folks, who personally experienced that revival and he also grew up in that community. What inspiring sermons and a call to get ourselves ready, should the Lord see fit to pour out His blessings upon us. The sermons truly were rousing, some of them lasting over 2 hours, with not one complaint being uttered from the congregation. The spirit of the Lord evident in the stillness and a sense of holiness and awe which seemed to permeate the air, lingering long after the service had finished.

After a lovely final service culminating in the Lord's Table it is then time to dismantle out stall and say our sad farewells to all our dear friends for yet another year. I am still amazed at the swift passage of time—things and events come and go so quickly. It is comforting to be able to say to our friends "God willing, see you next year. If not, see you in glory!" So it's never really goodbye because ultimately we WILL see each other again.

We look back over the years with such fondness and love for all the folks that have befriended us here. We remember with gratitude the incredible teaching and exposition of God's word that we have received and feel so blessed to be a part of this convention.

Chapter 17

Over the Sea to Skye

The weekend after the convention we still stay in Buckie as Gavin usually preaches in a church in Gardenstown the following Sunday.

We normally take the Saturday to relax after a busy week at the convention. Sometimes we would drive to the city of Elgin where we do some "retail therapy" which no woman can do without! It is lovely taking a quiet stroll through the main street. Yes, quiet, because the main street is closed to traffic and there are pavement cafés on the sidewalks with street musicians. So very different from going into the middle of Johannesburg or Pretoria! There you find nothing but noise from traffic jams and filth strewn streets from the many vendors who build make shift stalls on the pavements.

Gardenstown is fondly known as "Gamry". I do not know why this is so but all the locals call the town Gamry. The same is true for Findochty, which the locals call Fenechty, all for reasons totally unknown! Donald and his wife Suzanne (the minister of the church) often invite us to lunch so we have a lovely afternoon of sharing around God's Word before the evening service. It's amazing how small the world actually is and how God's people are all connected. Earlier I mentioned a most unlikely Free Church minister named Lachie who lives on the Isle of Uist. Lachie's wife and Donald's daughter are best friends.

Gavin preaching at The Gardenstown New Church.

Last year's meeting at Donald's church went especially well. I don't understand why, but some meetings seem so much more meaningful and special than others. The response of the congregation to us also plays a major role in this and Sunday night was indeed one of those really special meetings. There was coffee and tea after the service and while chatting with folks I heard someone greet me in Afrikaans. What a lovely surprise to meet a very pleasant young couple from the Netherlands. Estee's parents are Afrikaans South Africans who went to the Netherlands as missionaries. She had recently married a Dutch national and had taught him to speak Afrikaans, so we had a delightful conversation in that language. We had been away from South Africa for many months and the conversation made us feel homesick.

After the service we made the long drive back to Buckie. It was after midnight when we fell into bed utterly spent after a hard days "giving out". The next day we were up early, packed the car once again, and headed off to the Isle of Skye.

Last year it was pouring with rain and I got literally drowned in freezing water while loading the car. Graeme was most concerned and urged us to stay longer with them as there were reports of closures of many roads due to flooding. The torrential rain was forecast to continue for a few days and we were concerned that things would only deteriorate further and then we would perhaps miss our next meeting on Skye the following evening. So it was with some trepidation that we undertook the journey in this awful weather. Thankfully, although the conditions were very bad in some parts with roads totally under water we did not have to turn back and finally made it to our destination. We drove part of this route, back in June, on our way to the Uists and things looked remarkably different then. The green hills were now one mass of purple haze as the heather was in full bloom. Gone was the snow that capped the mountains, replaced now by many, what is usually, little streams that flow gently down the sides of the mountains.

But this time the streams had disappeared and in their place were seething masses of furious white rapids raging down the mountains at incredible speeds. It was quite something to behold. Whereas the last time we drove here I remarked on the beauty of God's creation, this time I stood in awe of His power and might.

The Isle of Skye is connected to mainland Scotland via a short causeway and a lengthy bridge. No more ferry crossing—hooray! We actually stay in Kyle of Lochalsh which is on mainland Scotland and then use the bridge when we need to cross over to Skye. In our early years of coming to Skye, we had to pay a toll to cross the bridge. Once the bridge was paid for the toll was done away with, which to us was a good thing for the locals.

One year, coming back from the Isle of Lewis to Uig on Skye, we received a message from one of our Pastor friends asking us to return to Lewis for an extra meeting. As it is expensive to take the car on the ferry, we decided to go back to Lewis as foot passengers. It was just overnight so shouldn't have been a problem. We did so and all went well, with us returning the next day to our vehicle, which we had left parked on the pier.

When Gavin tried to start the car, we discovered that the battery was flat! By this time it was evening and Uig, being a tiny hamlet, everything was shut. We had no choice but to spend the night in the car.

It was freezing cold, and because of our luggage we couldn't put the seats back, so had to try and sleep sitting up. I was so cold that I took a track suit top and wrapped it around my head and had my hands under my arm pits. Although wearing two pairs of socks, I couldn't work out why my feet were so cold and actually felt wet. Then I realised that the condensation on the inside of the windows, was running down in little droplets and landing on my feet. It was one of the most uncomfortable nights that I can ever remember!

Early the next morning, we were awakened by the sound of a large vehicle's engine running. There, coming down the road towards the pier was a huge AA truck. Gavin quickly got out of the car and went over to the driver of the truck. After explaining to the driver that we had a flat battery he promptly offered his help. He jump-started our car in no time and with a friendly wave went on his way. The AA became to us Aiding Angels that morning.

Another time, also coming back from Lewis, I caught some kind of virus and wasn't well. We were headed for Glasgow but I felt too ill to continue the journey and so we stopped in at Kyleakin for the night. We asked the Lord to show us a B&B, as we had not booked anywhere, not expecting to stay over. We came across a lovely little B&B and after knocking on the door and being warmly welcomed in we chatted with our hostess for a while.

Jess Anne revealed that she was a Christian and invited us to a prayer meeting later that evening. As I was feeling ill, I really didn't feel like going but felt obligated as we had been invited, so it was probably the right thing to do. Just after we arrived at the prayer meeting, who should walk in but a Pastor friend of ours from Broadford! At that time, we did not know that Broadford and Kyleakin were linked charges. We had only ever been to the Broadford Church.

Here was the start of a wonderful association with the Kyleakin Church of Scotland that has lasted for many years. They have been such a blessing and encouragement to us. Their prayer meetings are unique and special and one feels the Spirit of the Lord very keenly when they gather.

We have some really dear friends there now. Agnes and John took us under their wing and looked after us many times after that. We got on so well with John and had lively conver-

A like minded Christian brother, John with his wife Agnes.

sations with him. After a lovely visit a few years ago, six weeks later we received the news of his very sudden, tragic passing. We still visit Agnes and often reminisce with her about John and our lovely times together.

Currently we are hosted by Willy whom we met for the first

time last year. Not having met Willy before staying with him, we were not sure what to expect. Willy turned out to be a most gracious host and is starting to become a good friend. He is a bachelor who lives in a lovely little cottage two doors down from his folks. He has all his meals with them so we have the place largely to ourselves. Our room is spacious and there is even a desk for me to sit at and work on my cards as I usually sell out at Keswick. So much for my fears before meeting new folks; why can I not learn to trust my Saviour more? My apprehensions have always proven to be worse than the reality. Thank you dear Lord for your wondrous provision once again.

While chatting to Willy last year, we discovered another family connection that we had not been aware of. Willy is the first cousin of another very dear and close friend of ours. Ivor and Rosemary MacDonald, whom we met on Lewis on our very first visit there in 1995, have been close to us ever since then. Rosemary and Willy are first cousins and Rosemary's mother and Willy's mother are sisters.

We stay for a week in Klyle of Lochalsh. While there, in addition to other services, we have a meeting in the Kyleleakin Church of Scotland on the Tuesday night where we share about the work in South Africa, and then Gavin preaches there on the Sunday which is another wonderful blessed time of ministry. It's great to see some familiar faces but also enjoy meeting new ones. A few travellers attended our last meeting as well, which is unusual. For those of you who are perhaps not familiar with this term, these are people who at one time would have been called Gypsies.

During our stay with Willy last year we had tea with his

parents and disabled brother 2 doors down. What a lovely couple, they were such a blessing to us. Oh that I could grow old like that. As outward appearances change and beauty fades with age, I pray that the Lord would shine through me as He does through Mina (Willy's mother). Her femininity and outward beauty is eclipsed by the inner peace and grace that flows from within her. Her gentleness and patience are so evident in her dealing with her disabled adult son. Hardships in life truly do build character as evidenced here.

Alistair (her husband) had renal cancer and was suffering so, but not one word of complaint slipped from his lips. When we said our goodbyes to Mina and Alistair, it was particularly difficult because we knew that this would probably be the last time we would see Alistair due to his illness. Two weeks later, Alistair went home to glory.

Willy arranged a first time meeting in his church last year which is the Free Church of Kyle of Lochalish. The minister was away but Willy looked after us and things ran smoothly. We were invited back again so that bodes well for the future.

We celebrate our wedding anniversary while on the Isle of Skye. Where oh where have all the years gone? It feels just like yesterday that I was a fresh faced teenager instead now a rather mature or should I say "old" woman?

We try to plan to go somewhere special, but it doesn't always work out that way. The weather doesn't always allow us to do something involving outdoors. One year, it was chucking it down" (raining) as they say here and so sightseeing was out of the question. We decided to go into the "capital" of Skye which is a town called Portree. We were going to have lunch in the town before returning home. When we arrived the whole place was without electricity and so businesses closed their doors and there was absolutely nothing to do. We found out later that the whole of northern Scotland was without power due to some major fault. The electricity only came back on around 3 pm by which time we were rather hungry! We had our meal at a local tourist centre and then headed home. Nothing grand and nothing exciting!

The World Pipe Band Championships also take place while we are on Skye. They last two days, a Friday and Saturday. In years passed we would make every effort to get down to Glasgow to see it, come rain or shine. (Most often rain!) We would often get up at four in the morning to drive the long way from Buckie, Skye or where ever we found ourselves, down to Glasgow, to be there for the 10 am start. I remember years of sitting in the grandstands under an umbrella being soaking wet with the water from the brolly dripping down my neck. So glad those days are over! Oh, how I praise God for modern technology. The World's (as it is called) is now streamed live and so Gavin sits firmly ensconced behind his computer for 2 solid days watching the competition. It never ceases to amaze me how he can so accurately predict the winners but I suppose that this comes from years of practice, judging competitions in South Africa.

In years gone by, when we would attend the World Pipe Band Championships, Gavin would sometimes wear his kilt. He so looked the part of a true Scot, that tourists would often take his photograph!

As mentioned earlier, Gavin also preaches in Broadford on

a Sunday morning and then Kyleleakin on the same evening. I do the children's talk in the morning as well. The last time I spoke to the children about how a pearl is formed in an oyster. How uncomfortable it is for the oyster when the grain of sand rubs against its soft inner body and as the oyster coats that grain of sand, a beautiful pearl is formed. So it can be with us, that those things which are unpleasant and hurtful in our lives can be taken and turned into something very beautiful and precious to our Lord. Both services are well attended and a blessed time of worshipping our Lord is had by all.

Chapter 18

"Donald, Where's Yer Troosers?"
Glasgow

The drive down to Glasgow from Skye can be long which takes most of the day and is often uneventful. Mind you, not all the journeys down to Glasgow have been so.

One year it was particularly cold and there was snow and ice everywhere. It was beautiful and looked like a winter wonderland. We drove slowly through Glencoe and Gavin told me to look out for deer. He said that because the landscape was awash in snow, the deer should stand out in contrast to the pristine white that surrounded us.

We came to a layby on the side of the road where there seemed to be an unusual amount of vehicles parked. Gavin pulled into the layby to see what was happening. There in amongst the cars was one lonely looking wild Stag. He was causing quite a sensation and yet he didn't seem afraid and casually stood his ground. Most people returned to their cars after watching the Stag for a while and continued on their journey.

We waited until there was almost no one around and then I slowly inched closer and closer, until eventually I reached out my hand and was able to touch this wild beautiful creature. It is one of my most favourite memories.

Surprised by the fearlessness of the wild deer.

Back in the early 1990's when we first started coming to Scotland, Jacqui, the chairperson of the board of trustees in the UK, arranged accommodation for us in Kirkintilloch. We were due to stay for two weeks; the first week, with a couple whom we had never met before and the second week, with the local minister. We felt it was very brave of Gregor and Isobel to welcome two complete strangers into their home and put them up for a whole week but we were warmly welcomed and soon felt at home.

After a few days, Gregor and Isobel urged us not to move over to the minister but to stay the entire two weeks with them. This we did and it was the start of a very precious relationship that exists to this day. Every year, for fifteen years, we stayed with Gregor and Isobel. The two weeks eventually stretched in to six and they graciously put up with us.

A few years ago, Gregor was taken seriously ill with renal failure which finally ended his life. His funeral was a testimony to the stature of the man. The extremely large church was overflowing with friends and family, all saying a tearful goodbye. We know that we will see Gregor one day, restored to full strength and vigour, in glory. He was a wonderful man and we miss him greatly.

We were hosted by Rod and Alison two years ago for six weeks while they were living in Airth, Falkirk. That was the first year we had to look for accommodation in the Glasgow area after Gregor took so ill. We tried to find somewhere to stay, but for one reason or another, every door seemed to shut in our faces.

We were due in the Glasgow area in two days' time for a stay of six weeks, but still had no accommodation. I was beside myself, not knowing what we would do or where we would land up. We had prayed hard and couldn't understand why so many doors had closed to us. It was then that Gavin remembered that the previous year a lovely couple from the Falkirk Church of Scotland had offhandedly stated that if ever we needed a place to stay, their door was open to us. We felt rather embarrassed as Gavin phoned up asking if perhaps they could put us up for a few days while we continued to look for alternate accommodation. They graciously agreed and welcomed us with open arms.

We learned that Roderick had just finished training to be a pastor and had applied for a position in a nearby charge. A rather weighty document was sent to him, to be filled in on all manner of theological questions. This gave Gavin an opportunity to sit with Roderick discussing the many issues in question. We believe the Lord closed the door to all other avenues to force a situation so Gavin could aid Roderick. It turned out to be a blessed time. After the first week in their home, Rod and Alison insisted we stop looking for alternate accommodation and stay as long as needed.

Since they had moved into a smaller apartment, we did not stay with them the following year. Rod was inducted into the Drumchapel Baptist Church last year, and subsequently has moved into the manse. Once again they have kindly offered to host us should the need arise. How grateful I am to such welcoming folks who are willing to put up with us for so long.

The following year we needed to find alternate accommodation again, and although we had known Christine and David for many years, we had not stayed with them before. Their two adult sons "flew the nest" and the whole upstairs of their home became vacant. They therefore offered us the use of the upstairs of their home.

We were not sure what to expect when we arrived, but oh—to what lengths these dear people went to on our behalf. We stayed in 5-star luxury. I told David that they would have trouble getting us to leave when the time came; he just laughed and said the only time he would worry was if a crate arrived with my little pooch in it.

Our longest supporting Christian friends, David and Christine.

We had a huge room which was semi-divided into two. On one side of the room was the bed and cupboards. The other side was a mini-sitting room. It had a flat screen TV, two reclining chairs, the one electric, so Gavin could put his feet up. We had a DVD and a CD player. Next door was the bathroom for our private use, and also a little study where I could make my cards. Inside the study they had put a bar fridge, kettle, toaster and other bits and pieces. This meant we could have breakfast and lunch up the stairs and just share dinner with them. That gave both parties a measure of privacy as well. It could not have worked out better.

It is an absolute delight to unpack all our suitcases while in Glasgow. That is something that does not happen often. To have a cupboard has taken on new meaning and it is wonderful staying in one place for 6 weeks.

We have a busy time in the Glasgow area and our diary fills up fast with networking and social engagements as well. We sometimes find ourselves in a situation, like we did last year, of being out 23 nights in a row. Since we are getting older this is becoming increasingly difficult.

We have other wonderful friends, Frank and Christine who take us out to eat often. Our favourite restaurant is a Chinese buffet and many delightful hours have been spent in there with Frank and Christine. One year we had a telephone call from Frank. "I have terrible news for you," he said. "What?" we cried in alarm. "Our Chinese is closing!" came the pitiful wail from the other end of the phone line.

Frank is a director of Revival Radio and one of our delights is being interviewed on the radio which he graciously does while we are here. Frank is also on the board of Trustees for Rose of Sharon in Scotland. He and Christine have become dear friends and allies, and Frank has taken on arranging quite a few meetings for us over the years. They have a beautiful little West Highland Terrier named "Cushy" and so I am able to top up on doggy kisses and cuddles too. Frank "lets us loose" on his congregation each year before we head off to the radio station for the afternoon.

I forewarn my sister Heather, as she sometimes is able to listen via the internet for the afternoon. I even got to dedicate a piece of music to her last year. We have such lovely afternoons of being interviewed and talking about the work in South Africa and sharing about our faith. It is a wonderful opportunity to talk to so many people at once about the awesome God we serve.

Being interviewed at Revival Radio Studio.

Sundays are busy and we usually leave home by 9am returning around 10 pm. We arrive back tired but with a wonderful sense of satisfaction.

I remember the first time we had a meeting in Crossford Church of Scotland. We took a wrong turning and eventually had to stop and ask for directions. With our accent we would pronounce Crossford with the accent on the Cross thereby saying "CROSSfid." No one knew of such a place until eventually one man said "Oh- you mean CrissFORD!" It's amazing how changing one little accent on a word can make it unrecognisable.

We had a similar incident up north where the local dialect of Doric is spoken. We were looking for the Church of Scotland manse, and asked the postman for directions. He looked at us blankly and so we explained it was the house where the minister lived. His face brightened and he answered, "You want the Maaahhnse!" Sometimes our accents can make life a little more interesting.

We sometimes get bad news from home which can be distressing but the work needs to continue in spite of how we are feeling. Last year my sweet little Whisper came running into Heather's home with wet feet and slipped on the tiled floor and fell down the stairs. She snapped the tendon in her knee and surgery was scheduled for the following week. The vet said that it would take months to heal and that she would not be fully recovered by the time we arrived home in November. This, of course, upset me greatly. But I knew that she was in good hands as Heather loves her the way we do and would look after her in the best possible way.

Later in the week we were bemoaning the fate of little Whisper to another minister friend of ours who went on to tell us that his little dog had cataracts removed from both eyes at a huge cost. Talking about Whisper's operation—I was a "basket case" the day of her operation and was not able to concentrate on anything. I was constantly pleading to the Lord on behalf of our little puppy dog. Thankfully, Whisper's surgery was a success and was not as expensive as originally thought. A big thank you to Heather; for footing the bill. We could never have afforded the care for Whisper that Heather paid for. Whisper recovered remarkably well and Heather said that in no time she was already trying to put a little weight on that leg.

Unfortunately, a short while later Whisper fell desperately ill and was in doggie ICU for 3 days. Because of the operation on her leg and her arthritis, she had been given anti-inflammatory tablets and we suspect that this is what caused her bleeding ulcer. Of course one can never know for sure what causes these things but the poor wee mite really went through the mill. She was dehydrated and refused to eat.

The vet was talking about force feeding her, but thankfully at the last minute she ate a chicken leg and had some milk for lunch. We were ecstatic at the news. She saw the vet every day for nearly a week and my poor sister paid out literally thousands of Rand on our little treasure. But as Heather herself says, no price can be put on the value of our beloved pets that become like children to us. They are far more valuable than all the gold in the world. We are so grateful to Heather who has done a sterling job of caring and nursing Whisper. Apparently the house looked like a dispensary with a huge array of medicines which had to be taken at various times during the day. I will forever be grateful to Heather for the level of care and love shown to our little gem.

We average four meetings per week when in this area and then social and networking engagements added on top of that. In between this I frantically make as many cards as possible. The little bit of stock I manage to make gets snapped up almost immediately.

Alistair and Jenny (the minister and his wife in Falkirk) have us over for dinner before our meeting in their church and once again it is a great time fellowship. The meetings here are always blessed ones, and as I mentioned the cards sell well.

There is a lady in that church who is also an avid card maker and every time she knows we are coming to the church, she does a "clear out" of her stock and passes on some card making supplies to me. I am most grateful for this and get a lot of use from her stock. Another friend in Belfast, Romayne, does the same and I thank God for these two wonderful ladies who help me so much. I would never be able to buy the materials that they so generously pass on to me.

Gavin attends a minister's fraternal in Anniesland in Glasgow at least once while we are in this area. As it's a "men only" affair, I am given a rare opportunity of "me" time and usually choose to be dropped off in the centre of Glasgow where I take my time ambling through the crowded streets, window shopping and drinking coffee.

Last year though I opted to be dropped off at Silverburn Shopping Centre. When this centre was built about three or four years ago, it was reputed to be one of the biggest in Europe. Whether that is still the case I do not know. Having never been there before I thought it might be rather interesting. It is big with huge, high ceilings and massive, wide walkways. I sat in a coffee shop for a long time just watching the people rushing about, and I felt so sad.

To me, Silverburn is a temple built to the god of materialism and people come to worship mammon here. It typifies what the world has become. It was one clothing shop after the next, reinforcing the worldly view that looks are everything and people are judged by their outward appearance. If only we could take a leaf out of God's book and judge the way

He does—by looking past outward appearances and into the heart. It was not the most pleasant of mornings and I doubt very much that Silverburn will see me again.

We always have dinner with David and Fiona before having a missions meeting in their church in Lesmahago every year. The meetings are blessed with a great turnout and a lively question and answer session at the end.

We met David and Fiona at Keswick in Buckie years ago. It was at a time that Gavin felt he was "out on a limb". He felt isolated in many of his beliefs until he met David. They immediately found common ground and David has become a mentor to Gavin. They are dearly loved by us. Abbeygreen Church of Scotland with her many congregants have a special place in our hearts. They are one of our biggest supporting churches and much work has been done through their generous giving. Many more cards are sold there too and so the frantic making of them continues.

We also have a missions meeting in Bishopbriggs and dinner with the missions secretary of the church. George and Sheena have been friends of long standing. We enjoy fellowship with them, but more importantly I have the all-important "doggie fix"! Their gorgeous King Charles terrier "Molly" and I were great pals. Afterwards, we then go to the church for the meeting which again is so often blessed that we are incredibly humbled by all we see the Lord doing. Unfortunately we have just heard the sad news of the passing of Molly. I will miss her very much.

Each year Nan (our retired doctor friend) and Isobel (the widow of Gregor, with whom we stayed for 15 years every

Getting a doggie fix with Molly.

year until his death 2 years ago) take me for a girlie morning out. We have a wonderful time of drinking coffee and looking around garden centres and just chatting about feminine stuff. I miss female company, so this is really special. I'm grateful to thoughtful ladies like these two who would do this just for me.

Saukie United Free Church is another of the churches we often visit. Our relationship with Graeme and Christine (minister and his wife at Saukie) is slowly deepening; each year that we go back it just gets better and better. One year, while ministering in their church, I spoke about Christians being the sweet aroma of Christ. Since then, each time we see Christine, she gives me a bottle of perfume. There are ladies out there that think of these personal items that bring me so much pleasure and I could never thank them enough for thinking of me. I feel spoilt and treasured by them all.

Wayne is the Pastor at Carrubbers Church in Edinburgh and his wife, Sarah, have been good friends since we met in 2001. Years prior to our meeting, we had been advised by many folks to try and make contact with Wayne. We always replied that this was something we simply would not do. God, in His good time, if it was in His plan, would bring us together.

In 2001, Wayne was one of the speakers at Keswick in Buckie. After the mission stall holders had finished setting up their stands, Wayne walked through the stalls looking at the various displays. He picked up one of our magazines and read it. Later that night, after the convention meeting, Wayne made his way through the crowed hall to our stall. His first words to Gavin were "Brother, you and I have so much in common, let's talk!" A wonderful relationship has developed since then.

Wayne has been not only a brother to us, but a knight in shining armour as well. Carrubbers congregation has opened their arms to us both and support the work each year. We are grateful the Lord saw fit to allow our first meeting. This way we know that it was God initiated, and not man.

Carrubbers is a very large church on the Royal Mile in Edinburgh, serving mainly the University students who come to Edinburgh to study. Parking is always a nightmare because of where Carrubbers is situated. Last year, we had lunch with Wayne, Sarah and the girls and spent the afternoon with them after which we had to drive into the city to the church. All the way there I was praying for parking. Not something I would normally do, but it's just so difficult if parking is not available as Gavin simply cannot walk far.

We followed Wayne into the city, and as we got close to the church he pointed out a parking place for Gavin, but Gavin refused it, saying it was still too far from the church. I was starting to panic as I really didn't know what we would do. We arrived outside of Carrubbers only to find a parking space right at the door.

As part of the service, Wayne wanted to interview us. He has done this in the past and it was very well received so he felt that people would appreciate it if he did it again. I do not feel comfortable in this kind of situation, as I like to think about the questions before giving an answer. However, Wayne feels an "off the cuff" answer is always best, so he refused to tell us what he had in mind to ask us. I cannot remember what I said, which may be a good thing because I can't worry about it now!

We also have mid-week meetings at Harper Memorial Church. This is a very interesting church. John Harper was an Evangelist who felt God calling him to America, however many people in Glasgow disagreed with him going. Nevertheless, John bought a ticket on the Titanic. As the ship was going down, it was reported that John Harper was going around telling people about Jesus and how to be converted. He gave his life jacket to an unconverted person because John said he knew where he was going after this life. When John died, the Harper Memorial Church was established in his memory. We shared there for the first time last year and were very kindly invited back again this year. It is very encouraging when people come up to us with questions from our presentation of the previous year. The folks at Harper remembered all we had shared and wanted an update. It always makes for a great meeting when people are so interested.

Gavin with our dear brother in Christ, Wayne.

On the third Thursday every September we are up at the crack of dawn since we have to drive a nearly two hour journey to Longniddry and arrive by 10 am. We have had an association with The Candle Light Club for at least 10 or 11 years.

Longniddry is south of Edinburgh and it's a very pretty little village. The Candle Light Club is a group of pensioners who gather for fellowship every 3 months and then have a meal at the local inn afterwards. When we arrived last year, the first thing we noticed was that there were no cars in the parking lot. Realizing that something was wrong, I went into the inn and asked where the Candle Light Club was being held. The response was one of total ignorance. I then phoned Janice, the convenor of the club, on her mobile phone, only to find out that I had the dates mixed up and the meeting was only the following week.

Not only that, but Janice and Ian, her husband, were in Barbados on holiday and I had woken them up in the middle of the night. How embarrassed and stupid I felt! We then had to climb back in our car and make the two hour journey back "home".

Janice is another of those wonderful supporting ladies who look after me personally. Janice sells a certain brand of face creams and toiletries and has always been most generous in passing on supplies to me.

We always visit our friends Matthew and Muriel in Glasgow. Matthew was the head of Mission Aviation Fellowship (MAF) in Scotland until he retired a few years ago. It is good to meet up with them as they have such insight and understanding of what it is like to be on the mission field. Matthew has given us valuable advice over the years which we have taken to heart and implemented in our work.

We very seldom get to do anything "touristy" but last year I pleaded with Gavin to take me to see the Kelpies. The Kelpies are the largest equine structures in the world standing over 30 meters tall. There are two of them and are mythical creatures, but to me, they are just two very beautiful horses. What amazed me is how the structures capture the essence of a horse. They are life-like and beautiful, rising majestically from the ground. The Kelpies were built on the banks of the canal in honour of all the horses that pulled the barges up the canal in times past. One can see them from the highway, but up close they are even more impressive.

A major tourist attraction: The Kelpies.

By the time our visit to the Glasgow area is drawing to a close, the nip of winter can be felt in the air. The nights are "drawing in", as they say here and it's dark by 8 pm. Such a change from the nights when the sun could be seen at 11 pm. The winter woollies start coming out, as does the electric blanket.

We usually start feeling not only physically tired now but also "people tired" and long for quiet time alone. It's not surprising as by this time we have been on the road for around seventeen weeks already, and the going is not always easy. We are definitely running on empty at this stage of our trip, but the Lord sustains us through it all.

My heart always feels heavy and I mourn the passing of our days in Scotland. I have come to love this land passionately and her people even more so. Glasgow is a home from home and it is here that I am at my happiest.

Chapter 19

Violence and Blessing: Ireland

B y the end of our stay in Glasgow, both Gavin and I are completely exhausted. Thankfully, although Ireland is busy, it's not so busy that we cannot catch our breath.

One of our biggest concerns when going to Ireland is the ferry crossing. We watch the weather report avidly hoping for no torrential rain or strong winds. We in the most part have survived the crossings with only a handful being really bad.

One year our ferry from the port of Troon was cancelled due to "adverse weather conditions" and we were forced to drive another 2 hours southwest to the port of Cairnryan to catch a ferry from there. It was a nightmare journey with heavy rain and poor visibility.

The ferry was jammed packed, filled to capacity due to all the extra passengers from the cancelled ferry. The crossing itself was reasonably calm and both Gavin and I suffered few ill effects.

Looking back over the years we have spent visiting Ireland, we have so many wonderful stories and memories. Of the three lads that Gavin met in China way back in the 1990's, Leonard has been the one who befriended us, who has looked after and supported the ministry and us personally. On our first visit to his beautiful farm, sitting chatting over a meal, I casually asked Leonard what he grew on his farm. He looked up and with a crooked smile and answered "milk!"

Gavin with Leonard whom he met in China.

The early years were spent in developing relationships with folks and various churches. It was a time of learning to understand the culture of the people and their way of doing things, which very often was different from ours.

Over all, the conservative evangelical wing of the Protestant church in Ireland is small. Yet, they generously welcomed us. At times, we have had to "pass muster" before being allowed to participate in some services. For example, we had been recommended to a church in Northern Ireland, who at the time didn't have a minister.

Gavin was asked to preach in the church on a Sunday evening. The day before, we received a telephone call from one of the elders who then proceeded to ask Gavin all manner of theological questions. After answering all the enquiries, the elder then replied, "Well, Mr Campbell, that's fine. But I must warn you, that if you deviate from anything that you have said this afternoon, we will have to escort you from the pulpit."

The next day, with not a little trepidation, we arrived at another of the elder's homes just before the service. As I have said many times, my husband tends to stand out from the crowd due to his large frame and his appearance. He would wear loud, bright African shirts to preach in and he gained a reputation for doing this. He would also wear his big silver cross around his neck. In some conservative circles, we never knew if his appearance might cause offence and this was one of those incidents. He had inadvertently left his cross at home, but here we stood, with him in a bright African shirt and me with makeup and nail polish, not sure whether we would be accepted or not.

The elder answered the knock on his door and cautiously invited us in. His wife came up behind him with a look of recognition on her face smiled and exclaimed, "Gavin! Where's your cross?" The dear lady had been in a previous meeting of ours but had not made the connection until she saw us. We had the most wonderful, blessed time of fellowship together and a glorious meeting.

Stephen is the Pastor of the Dundalk Baptist Church. He and his wife Mari have been friends of ours for about 10 years. The church folks have always been most welcoming and we have a fellowship lunch afterwards which is always lovely. Some folks in these churches, as is the case with Stephen and Mari, come out of a Catholic background and still have family who are of the Catholic faith.

One year, we had another meeting scheduled for mid-afternoon in the Iron Church in Carnaross, after the Fellowship lunch with the Dundalk folks. Carnaross is quite a distance away and I worked out that we should leave around 2 pm. I looked at the clock on the wall and noticed that it was before 1 pm and thinking we had plenty of time, had a lovely leisurely lunch.

After our meal, I casually glanced at the clock again, only to see that the clock hands were still pointing to just before 1 pm. With blind panic I looked at my wrist watch and in horror saw that it was well after 2 pm and if our calculations were correct, we were running about an hour late. Oh dear! We hastily said our goodbyes and literally hit the road at some speed.

We telephoned our friend Leonard and explained the situation. He reassured us that Irish time is very laid back and the 3:30 pm starting time of the service would likely be closer to 4 pm. He also said that they would keep the congregation singing favourite hymns until we arrived. We had a nightmare journey, racing through tiny back lanes and winding farm roads, finally arriving just ten minutes late.

The Iron Church, Pastor and congregants have been very good to us over many years. The small Sunday school collects coins during the year and then presents them to us when we arrive. This we use specifically for the Sunday Schools in South Africa. It is a wonderful gesture of children helping other children.

Unfortunately, the sectarian violence which has plagued Ireland as a whole for many decades now, seems to raise its ugly head every so often. An Orange Order hall was burnt down and a Presbyterian Church was set alight (using the Bible as the catalyst!) near Raphoe in the north on our last trip. A pipe bomb was found near Belfast and a huge cache of arms was found on a farm in County Fermanagh as well. It is sad as this is such a beautiful country with many wonderful people.

I remember a few years ago when the violence was severe and we were travelling from the Republic up into the north for a meeting. We entered one of the towns on the border, which almost straddles both north and south. There had been a protest march not long before our arrival, and we came across a huge articulated vehicle stranded across the middle of a main intersection. It was burning furiously and the traffic lights above the lorry were bowing down towards it as they slowly melted from the heat. There were rocks strewn in the road and the place looked a horrible mess. My darling husband decided against all my pleas not to do so, stopped the car, jumped out and started taking photographs. Some local folks noticed this and started cat-calling and eventually picked up stones and commenced pelting Gavin with them. Needless to say this caused a hasty retreat and we sped away quickly.

On another occasion, returning home in the early hours one morning from a late meeting in the north, we were heading south in a car bearing southern Irish number plates. We had passed a number of smouldering vehicles on the side of the road with hurriedly made sign posts with all manner of political slogans. Suddenly, we saw blue flashing lights behind our vehicle. It was a police van indicating for us to pull over. This we dutifully did and two policemen hurriedly got out of their car; one ran to the opposite side of the road and dropped down on one knee aiming an automatic rifle at us. The other policeman came over and asked where we were travelling to at such a late hour and why. After hearing our accents, they both visibly relaxed and gladly left us to complete our journey.

Accommodation in Ireland was never a problem for many years. We used to stay on a farm in Enniskillen with some dear friends there. Eventually our hosts Father passed away and her Mother came to live in the accommodation that we had enjoyed for about 15 years.

We then had to start looking for accommodation, which was not always forth coming. One year we were given the use of a beautiful little cottage while the owner was away on holiday. We had arranged to spend the last week end of our stay in Ireland with friends a distance away. We had been instructed that when we were ready to leave the cottage, to post the keys through the letterbox in the front door. After cleaning the house and packing the car, we duly posted the keys as instructed.

As we neared our next port of call, we received a frantic message from our friends stating that they had had a medical emergency and could no longer have us stay. We then had to find a hardware store, where we bought a doweling rod, a magnet and some string. We went back to the little cottage and began "fishing" through the letter box. If a policeman had passed by the house we would have been arrested for house breaking! Finally after much struggling, not being able to see the key, the magnet caught the tiny ring holder and we managed to retrieve the keys and let ourselves back into the cottage once more.

Last year we had another problem with accommodation. It was eventually graciously provided through two missionaries working for New Tribes Mission in Indonesia. This year though, they have subsequently rented out that property, so it was no longer available. Our dear friend, Wayne, at Carrubbers Church in Edinburgh, came to the rescue once again. Wayne is good friends with the pastor of the Portadown Baptist church (in the town we stayed in last year) and we attended a service there last October. Anyway, John (the Portadown pastor) has kindly offered for us to have a meeting in his church in October this year. Two congregants of his have a cottage in Dungannon that they are willing to allow us to use. God is so good and does supply all our needs. When I think of all the answered prayer, I stand back in awe and wonder.

We have a missions meeting in the village of Drum each year. It is a fair journey from Portadown where we stayed last year and it took about an hour and a half to drive there. The scenery was stunning. Ireland is so green, with tall hedges coming right up to the sides of the road; the autumn colours of the leaves on the trees, standing out in stark contrast to the rich green colour of the grass. There are stone walls that checker the landscape, where cows and sheep graze lazily on the lush vegetation. The distinctive smell of slurry in the air is the only mar on the landscape, but we are getting used to that very potent smell.

When we arrived in Drum, Cecil (who arranged for us to be there) was most apologetic explaining that he had double booked. The representative from another organization was most adamant that he could not come another day, which left us having to bow out gracefully. We promised to return in two weeks' time. So we turned around and drove home again.

Two weeks later we returned for the meeting. Before attending the gathering we went to visit Cecil's wife. Cecil and Iris have been supporters of Rose of Sharon for many years.

Unfortunately, Iris developed cancer about two years ago and we had not seen her for all that time. It was good to see her and catch up after so long. It is sad to see so many of our dear friends struck down with this awful disease.

The Corwillis Prayer group in Drum is a small one, but a delight. On the way home there was a detour due to road works, but for some reason after the first road sign showing the detour, all signs disappeared. Our Sat Nav was having none of this and refused to accept any other way home. It kept insisting on taking us back to the road that was now closed. We got totally lost in the middle of the night on small winding back roads in the middle of nowhere. It was 1 am before we finally found our way back to Portadown.

We spend a week end in Castlebar each year which is about 250 kilometres from where we were staying in Portadown last year. Cathal and Sharon too, befriended us way back in 1995 and Cathal is the Pastor of the church in Castlebar. We met

Cathal and Sharon when they were still in Coothill. We remember wonderful times of fellowship and of shared meals there, before they transferred to Castlebar.

Once settled in Castlebar, Cathal graciously introduced us to this fellowship. We drive there on a Saturday morning and spend time with them in the afternoon, catching up on all the news from the past year. We occasionally sleep over with a South African lady, Dawn, whom we have known for a few years. It is good to hear the familiar accent after so many months away from home. The meetings are always a pleasure and it is encouraging to have so many people interested in what the Lord is doing in South Africa.

Pastor Cathal and Sharon from Castlebar.

We also have a meeting in the Ardahee Prayer Fellowship which is usually far from where we stay. It is strange that although Letterkenny is way up in the north of Ireland it is considered as being "in the south" because it is part of the Republic of Ireland. It is a long way to go for a small meeting, but we are reminded that it's not always about numbers or distance, but about doing God's work.

We still pray daily that He would use us to bless, challenge and encourage His people and we believe that He has answered that prayer. The meeting in Ardahee usually finishes rather late and by the time we arrive home it is nearly 2 am, so another late night once again.

We have been so encouraged to see the growth in Athlone Baptist Church. We have been visiting this church for the past 20 years and have watched the ebb and flow of folks coming and going. This year the church was jammed-packed with not a seat to be had. We don't find that very often here and it was a pure joy to see. Athlone is one of our longest supporting churches and we are so grateful to them for their loving kindness. The pastor, Dominic, and his wife Carol, have fed us, loved us and blessed us over the many years of our association with them. We take deep pleasure in our relationship with the Athlone Baptist Church and thank God for them.

Dominic and Carol used to have an old dog of uncertain parentage who loved stones. I would spend copious amounts of time picking up stones and throwing them for the dog. He would gaily tear after them and bring back a warm slimy stone covered in doggie saliva pleading for me to throw it again. Poor wee mite has since passed onto doggie glory but is still fondly remembered.

At one point in our travels we came to a three way inter

Pastor Dominic and family in Athlone.

section. Through the rain and inky blackness of the night we spotted a little dog strolling aimlessly in the middle of the intersection. I was absolutely horrified as this poor little thing was in imminent danger of being run over. Gavin drove to the middle of the intersection, put on his hazard flashes and I jumped out of the car in the pouring rain and tried to catch the unfortunate animal. As I approached the little thing, it seemed oblivious to my presence and didn't even try to run away. When I picked him up, he showed the first indication of a fright and I wondered to myself if this doggie was perhaps blind.

I bundled the soaking ball of fur in my jersey and hopped back in the car. There was an inn at this busy intersection and we decided to go in there to see if we could find the dog's owner. We asked all the staff and the patrons, but no one seemed to know or recognise the animal. Suddenly the chef appeared and he said that he thought he knew who the owners were. After a few phone calls the owners were tracked down and promised to come immediately to fetch their pet.

It turned out that this sweet little bundle of fluff was sixteen years old, blind and deaf. He had inadvertently got out of his yard and was wondering aimlessly about. The folks arrived and there was a happy reunion between beloved pet and owner.

Later that evening Gavin said that he had been thinking about the little dog and came to the conclusion that we are very similar to it. Before our conversion to faith in Jesus, we are in mortal danger of losing our souls and are in a sense blind and deaf to the Lord's calling. The sad part of this is that we don't even realise the danger we are in. It's only when our eyes and ears are opened to the Gospel message of Christ and we respond to it that the danger is diverted and we are saved, just like that little hound.

Some years we have had problems getting our very necessary medication. Deanne posts the medicines to us on a monthly basis. Unfortunately, we do have postal strikes and when that happens there is always an anxious time of waiting and praying that we don't run out of medication for life threatening conditions. These include Gavin's heart medication, diabetic medicine, high blood pressure and cholesterol medication.

It is difficult having to self-medicate while travelling for so many months, and a postal strike just adds to an already stressful situation. The packages that do arrive from South

Africa containing our medication have all been slit open by customs and are thoroughly checked before being passed on to us. This is a good thing, and we don't mind at all, as we have been proven not to be drug smugglers.

After a month of intense ministry we leave Ireland amazed at the doors the Lord has unlocked for us, the homes he has opened, and the people He has brought across our path. We feel honoured and privileged to be able to do this work. Yes, it's tough and hard going and at times; one feels homesick, discouraged and exhausted, but all in all I wouldn't have it any other way!

Chapter 20

Into the Wilds of London

We left in the early hours of a Monday morning to travel to Belfast to catch the ferry back to Scotland. We arrived in Cairnryan and then drove down to North Yorkshire which took the rest of the day. We arrived in Amotherby, in North Yorkshire, around 8 pm that night. It was incredibly tiring, since we went to bed late the night before after cleaning the house where we stayed and loading the car.

We met John and Mary Waller in Israel in 1995 when we were visiting Gavin's brother there. They befriended us and invited Gavin and I to visit them in Hull the following year, which we did. We have been firm friends ever since.

John was the vicar of the minster in Hull and a lovely, gentle Christian man. Sadly, John passed away two years ago after struggling with Alzheimer's disease for about two years.

We still keep in touch with Mary and visit her annually on our way down south. We went to Hull the next day to visit another friend, Vivienne, who we originally met in John's Church in 1996. We had a valued relationship with Vivienne and looked forward to seeing her. We started the drive south to Hull after saying a fond farewell to Mary.

Mary, Vivienne and the late Rev John from Hull.

Yorkshire has to be one of the prettiest counties in England. It comprises the Cotswolds which are well-known from the writings of James Herriot. For those of you who may not have heard of him, he wrote beautiful and funny stories about his life as a country veterinarian in the Yorkshire dales just after the Second World War. The area is pretty and is all one imagines rural England to be; rustic with quaint cottages, rolling hills and cattle and sheep grazing idly in green pastures. Silly names for little villages such as Spittle and Shitten dot the landscape. It is a very pleasant drive southward.

We stayed in the suburb of Hessle (part of the city of Hull) with Vivienne and it's always a joy to see her again and catch up on family news. The next day we attended the Hessle mid-week prayer meeting and had coffee with the parishioners after the service. We didn't do much other than visit with Vivienne. After that, we took our leave of her and drove further south to Stowmarket, which takes us the best part of four hours to do.

We arrived on the farm in Stowmarket around lunch time and were once again met by our good friends. We spend the afternoon chatting and catching up on all their news before heading to the caravan. Then, I began the huge task of unloading the car completely, unpacking the suitcases, quickly doing a load of washing, and hanging the wet clothing over heaters to dry. After that, I had to repack a smaller suitcase to take with us into London.

As we must park on the street in London, it is not a good idea to leave articles in the vehicle. It's usually after midnight again before I was able to fall into bed. We had to get up early the next morning to do the final packing of last minute articles and toiletries, and then we "hit the road" for the three hour drive into London.

I have an irrational hatred of London. I can cope with most things and most cities, but London is where I draw the line. I suppose it all started many years ago before the days of Sat Nav, and before we were more familiar with the place. As Gavin cannot walk any distance, and refuses to use the Underground, the only way to get around is by car. I am the navigator and I would sit with a map on my lap giving directions.

Added to the complications of driving in a busy city, is my very bad habit of calling my right hand my left and vice versa. This comes from the years of teaching Ballet, when facing the children in the class everything had to be a mirror image for the students and therefore your right literally becomes your left. It is an extremely annoying and difficult habit to break. I would scream at Gavin to turn RIGHT while gesturing to turn left with my hands. No wonder the poor man often got confused! Driving in central London is an extremely stressful experience. The one-way systems are a nightmare and the congestion zone adds to the problems.

One year Gavin wanted to visit the Metropolitan Tabernacle where Charles Haddon Spurgeon had been the preacher. There is a wonderful Christian bookshop there in which Gavin takes great delight.

Because the church is on the other side of London from where we stay in the West end, one has to go through the congestion zone. We feel the charge for the congestion zone is very high and are reluctant to pay it. There is only one route that cuts through the heart of London where one does not have to pay the congestion charge. After carefully studying a map, we worked out a route which would take us to the Metropolitan Tabernacle without having to pay the charge. We set off fairly confident that we would find the way. What a mistake—it was a nightmare journey and we got hopelessly lost. We finally pulled into a supermarket parking lot and called a taxi to take us to the church. We then had to pay another taxi to return us to our car. When all was said and done, it cost us far more in taxi fares than if we had just paid the congestion charge to begin with.

Generally, people are impatient and traffic is heavy in London. Needless to say, I think I now have a phobia about the place. I find London dirty, noisy, smelly and overcrowded. There is nothing there that appeals to me. I have no inclination to go sightseeing or visit any shops. We are ideally situated to do this, staying as we do with our friend Barbara. Her apartment is in the west end of London, situated between Hyde Park and Paddington Station, with easy access to the heart of the city. But I would rather just stay put than venture out into that concrete jungle. Even the intense desire to visit my grandfather's home in Lambeth does not entice me from the safety of Barbara's flat!

The parking is horrendous. This is fast becoming a cashless society where even the roadside parking meters don't take coins anymore. Everything has to be paid for by way of a debit/credit card. One is only allowed to park for a maximum of 4 hours before having to move and look for another parking spot, so you are constantly aware of the time. The parking wardens are strict and hover over their designated spots just waiting for meters to expire, giving no leeway to offenders. The whole experience leaves me depressed with a deep desire to "escape".

It's lovely visiting with Barbara, however. We get on really well and have much in common. She spoils us rotten and her home is a haven, a port of call in a storm, so to speak. We also visit with another dear friend here in London, Belinda.

Belinda is a lovely unassuming, mature lady who also lives in the west end. She and her husband John are both artists and their large apartment is crammed full of weird geometric shapes and various art works hanging on the walls.

Our faithful friend Barbara.

As you can tell by my descriptions, I am by no means an art connoisseur and wouldn't have a clue as to what is considered "good art". Barbara is also an artist, but she paints what I would consider more realistic paintings and is selling quite a lot of her work now. Some of it is lovely.

In earlier years while in London, we stayed with another couple, Neil and Beverly. They had two lovely little dogs that we took great delight in visiting each year. Neil, being an opera singer, fittingly named his dog "Figaro". The name Figaro conjures up in one's mind a dog of some stature. Instead, Figaro turned out to be no larger than a rat. He was a Yorkshire terrier who had the heart of a lion. What he lacked in size he made up for in courage and personality.

Coco was Figaro's little companion and she was a Laso Apso, which is akin to little Whisper, so no guessing which dog I favoured. One day, Neil asked if we would like to take the two dogs for a walk in Hyde Park. We jumped at the opportunity and I had Coco on the lead while Gavin had little Figaro. The sight of a huge bulky man with a tiny rat sized dog on a lead made a funny picture.

As soon as Figaro spotted another dog, irrespective of size, he would want to attack the other animal. Barking furiously, Figaro would strain and pull on his lead and to make the already funny picture more hilarious, Gavin would playfully act as if Figaro was pulling him along and would shout, "Wait, stop, help!" The looks of utter astonishment on the faces of passers-by were hilarious.

On another trip to London, a friend offered us the use of her cottage in Devon for a few days break. It was the most charming character-filled little place being built in the 1400's. Unfortunately, the weather was inclement and eventually the rain became too much for us and we decided to return to London. Parking in the area was a problem and so our vehicle was parked a fair distance from the cottage. When the suitcases were packed and ready, Gavin went to fetch the car while I waited at the cottage.

He likes to tell what happened as he walked to the vehicle. A stooped little old lady, walking on the opposite side of the street, kept staring at him. Eventually she crossed the road and came over to him. She pointed to the cross around his neck and asked, "Excuse me sir," she said, "does that cross around your neck mean that you are a Christian?" "Not necessarily" replied my husband, "but I am a Christian" he added.

She then said, "Please sir, would you tell me about Jesus?" Gavin spent the best part of an hour with this dear soul, and after explaining the Gospel message to her she took him by the hand and led him to a big church.

"This is the church I have been brought up in, but I still did not understand about Jesus", she said. She later told Gavin that her children would make fun of her because she could not explain her beliefs to them. What a divine encounter, foreordained by our precious Lord, who cares for all His children.

Halloween is celebrated in a big way here, and it's a day I detest with a passion. I am sorry to learn that it is becoming quite popular in South Africa now. People see it as harmless fun, but if only they realised the dark spiritual forces behind their "harmless fun" they would be shocked and horrified.

St Helen's Gardens Anglican Church has been one of our supporting churches for many years. The vicar, Steve, lived in South Africa for 3 years so also has an understanding of the place.

After packing up at Barbara's, we load our few bits and pieces into the car before saying goodbye to her. Unfortunately, last year it was bucketing rain and I got absolutely soaked doing the packing. We arrived at St Helen's with my hair literally plastered to my head and my clothes dripping. Yes, we do have an umbrella but I cannot load and hold an umbrella at the same time. My raincoat was back on the farm as we had travelled light to London, so it was my own fault. I looked like a drowned rat at the meeting, but otherwise all went well. Towards the end of a trip like this I tend to catch a cold; I suppose it is bound to happen. After so many months on the road my immune system gets low. I normally lose my voice completely and this happened once again last year. I had a microphone, and by screaming at the top of my voice, I managed to make my hoarse little whisper loud enough for folks to hear.

After the meeting we had a church lunch and most people stayed. We were able to chat to many folks, and a good time was had by all. It was after 3 pm before we finally managed to get away. I watched London disappear into the distance with a sigh of relief as we made our way back to Stowmarket.

Chapter 21

Full Circle

So, after five and a half months of travel we came full circle, back to the caravan where our trip starts each year. In the early morning I often sit and contemplate all the Lord has allowed us to see and do. All is quiet in the caravan on the farm at this time of the morning, but the rasping call of the pheasants will start soon enough. Five months ago it was mild, with beautiful green grass and lush bushes, and bunnies hopping about by the gurgling nearby stream. Now, it's bitterly cold, the frost lying thick on the ground, the trees bare of leaves and no bunnies can be seen. But there is a stark beauty, and a peace and quiet that allows a person to feel Gods' presence.

On our last trip we decided to drive into Ipswich, which is my favourite English town. I love the architecture of the place and the winding little alleyways which lead to tiny quaint shops and eating houses. We needed to start closing our lives down in the UK and also wanted to purchase a few last minute bits 'n bobs.

It was exceedingly cold; the wind was strong, making it feel even colder than it was. As the main road is a "walk way," we had to park the car and go on foot. This is always difficult for Gavin, but we took it slowly and he managed.

Being so cold, we decided to pop into a coffee shop for some warmth. We both needed the bathroom, so I held Gavin's shoulder bag while he went in. When he came out I handed him his bag and then I went in. When I came out I found Gavin at a table, and as I sat down, I asked him where my handbag was. I thought that since I had held his bag for him, that I had given him my bag to hold. He denied that I had given it to him and then the panic started to set in.

Because we were in the process of closing down our lives in England, I had our passports, flight tickets, my identity document, driver's license and other things in my bag. My legs felt weak as the adrenaline pumped through my veins as I rushed back to the bathroom to look for my handbag. The end of the queue for ordering coffee was also at the door to the bathroom. I think everyone could see the look of blind panic on my face. To make matters worse, the toilet door was locked—someone was inside!

"My bag, my bag", I said loudly. A lady near the end of the queue said, "Yes, I know, I found it and handed it in behind the counter". To my utter relief, the sales assistant handed over my much-loved belonging. The gratitude I felt towards that lady was indescribable. I thanked her profusely for her honesty. I explained that our passports were in my bag and we would have been in a dreadful predicament if it were not for her integrity.

There was a man standing behind her in the queue and he piped up and said, "Lady, it's your lucky day!"

"No", I thought, it's not luck; it's the provision and protection of a loving heavenly Father who knows I would never have coped in that situation. How I thank God for His provision and protection. I'm thanking Him still.

Before heading back to South Africa, our hosts often take us out. It was no different on this trip. They took us to the small village of Laversham. This village was exceedingly wealthy at one time, being built on the proceeds from wool. Unfortunately, high taxes and cheap imports from the continent destroyed that wealth and Laversham fell on hard times. It sounds so familiar and up-to-date. Anyway, Laversham stayed in the shadows for hundreds of years because the people did not have the finances to improve or modernise their homes. The result is a picturesque English village where the vast majority of the houses are around five to six hundred years old. Wealthy people live there again. It is quaint and has become a tourist attraction.

We stopped at the village church first. What an experience we had! The original church building was completed in 1260 and was then replaced with the existing one in 1445. There is a list of all the ministers of that church going back to 1260 on an inside wall. It is an amazing piece of history.

I loved walking through the building, reading little stories of various people who have worshipped there through the ages. Not only is it steeped in history, but hundreds of years of worship have been offered up in that building. A keen sense of holiness hovers about the place. I looked at the intricate carvings of wood and wondered whose hands had carved those beautiful designs and what was their life like? I thought about every minister who had shepherded a flock there and wondered about their lives and times. It was a fascinating experience.

After that, we headed into the village centre and ate at a tiny restaurant that seats only 20 people. It's upstairs in a home that was built in the 1400's. Here too, on the wall, were the names of previous owners and their occupations. That little home, at one time or another, had been everything from a medical practitioner's home to a milliner's store. After a delicious meal we ambled through the village marvelling at the uniqueness of the place.

We had all the last minute arrangements to make before leaving UK shores. We had to take out a SORN statement on our car, which legally takes it off the road in Britain. Our host kindly allows us to park the vehicle on the farm until we return.

For five and a half months I have a hankering to go home, and then when the time finally arrives I get slightly hesitant. After living in the UK where there is relative peace and safety, the abnormal conditions in South Africa, with its violence and crime, requires a huge adjustment. It's hard to reconcile ourselves to that way of life. It is refreshing to see children in the UK having the freedom to play outside, young women pushing prams and folks walking their dogs with no fear of attack. Having no burglar bars on the windows is an absolute delight.

No heavy security gates or high electric fences gives a sense of peace and security. It takes time to readjust to living in an abnormal society where tension and fear is the norm.

Each year I have every intention of kissing every single hair off my beloved little Whisper's body, and I plan to keep her as close to me as possible. I cannot wait to see my much loved and missed daughter Deanne, my grandchild, my sister and my close friends. So with great expectation, trepidation and excitement, we make the long, tiring journey back home.

The first thing that strikes us when we land in South Africa is the tension in the air. People walk around looking over their shoulder. Women clutch their handbags. Everyone closely guards their possessions. High walls surround homes and they have burglar bars on all windows.

When you look into the distance, you see thousands upon thousands of tiny shacks dotting the landscape and you know the teeming masses are looking for something to eat. The scene is a far cry from where we just came from.

Nevertheless, it's marvellous to see the cloudless blue skies and feel the touch of the warm African sun upon my skin instead of the cold and damp of the UK.

The anticipation of reunion with Whisper and Heather grows with each passing mile as we get closer to the house.

Furious excited barking and shouting announces our arrival. As we walk through the door, Whisper goes berserk. Her excitement is so great she doesn't know what to do. She runs around in circles, and greets us with squeals of delight, her tail wagging furiously. Her wriggling little body is difficult to hold. She covers our faces with licks and she becomes very clingy and she keeps us in her sight from that moment on. It is a very precious reunion with an animal we look upon as one would a child, and our hearts burst with love.

It was wonderful to see Heather again and we shared hugs and indescribable joy. We spent time chatting, catching up on news and revelling in each other's company.

Over the following days we bought grocery hampers and sweets so we could do outreach along the road on our return journey to Pretoria. We also bought Christmas gifts and sweet hampers for the kiddies at Tiny Tots Day Care Centre, which we delivered amidst much excitement and exhilaration.

After we completed preparations, we said another round of sad farewells to Heather and doggie Klara, and we started the long two-day drive home. We met many sad cases along the road and did our utmost to bring a measure of relief to them. We gave funds, grocery hampers and Gospel tracts to the old folks, and pocket money, sweet hampers and Gospel tracts to the children.

As we got closer to Pretoria, our excitement increased as we thought of being in our own little home again surrounded by our personal creature comforts. We looked forward to sleeping in our own bed, eating our own style food (portion sizes of our choosing), and not having to constantly pack and unpack our belongings. It is hard to describe the feeling of relaxation that comes when you are in your own haven. The old saying is true—there is no place like home. The feelings of delight and contentment upon entering our abode were inexpressible.

We then began the laborious task of restarting our lives in South Africa. We had to reconnect telephones, the Internet, and buy our personal groceries and restock the ministry pantry. We had to sort through mountains of post and thoroughly clean our house which had been uninhabited for nearly six months.

Within a few days we bought bulk packs of sweets and groceries and packed hampers for the start of the Christmas Outreach.

On our first Saturday in Pretoria, Deanne came to visit. I awoke early with great excitement and expectation. I was like the proverbial "cat on a hot tin roof" not being able to sit still; I anxiously paced the house waiting for the buzzer at the gate to announce her arrival.

When the buzzer sounded, I flew out of the house because I was not able to contain myself. We clung to each other with laughter and tears. A precious and intimate moment of pure bliss ensued. Holding my daughter in my arms after a six month absence is one of the most intense feelings of love and gratitude I have ever known.

Then, there was another glorious reunion with little Mikayla who shyly greeted her Granny, whom she has all but forgotten in her very short life. The relationship takes time to build again, but as she grows older this becomes easier because she remembers better who I am.

So, the cycle begins over with the work in South Africa and all the people we are called to serve and minister to in our homeland. All too soon—six and a half months later—we return to the UK to repeat the trip we have just completed.

Epilogue

The saga continues. As we enter the winter years of our lives, people ask us when we are going to retire. Our answer is always the same: "Never!" Not having funds to call our own, with no pension and no savings, we will continue to work as long as we are able.

Gavin always says he will, "Die in the saddle." No matter what the future holds, I have no doubt that the stories will carry on and that, "He, who started a good work in me, will be faithful to complete it." (Philippians 1:6 New King James Version)

So dear friends, until that day He calls us home, or comes again, we shall work while there is still light. To Him be all praise, Glory and honour for ever, Amen.

Made in the USA
Charleston, SC
13 September 2016